PREEMPTIVE
BIDDING

PREEMPTIVE BIDDING

Bid More, Win More
Bid More, Lose Less

Robert B. Ewen

PRENTICE-HALL, INC., Englewood Cliffs, N.J.

I am indebted to Estee Griffin and Tom Smith for helping to make this book a reality; to *The Bridge World* (39 West 94th Street, New York, N.Y. 10025) for permission to use material from that technically excellent guide to better bridge; to Dick Frey for his wise advice; and to my friends and acquaintances in the world of bridge for supplying not only memorable hands but memorable experiences as well.

Preemptive Bidding: Bid More,
Win More, Bid More, Lose Less
by Robert B. Ewen
Copyright © 1975 by Robert B. Ewen

Printed in the United States of America

Prentice-Hall International, Inc., London
Prentice-Hall of Australia, Pty. Ltd., Sydney
Prentice-Hall of Canada, Ltd., Toronto
Prentice-Hall of India Private Ltd., New Delhi
Prentice-Hall of Japan, Inc., Tokyo

10 9 8 7 6 5 4 3 2 1

Library of Congress Cataloging in Publication Data

Ewen, Robert B
  Preemptive bidding.

  1. Contract bridge. I. Title.
GV1282.3.E923   795.4'152   75-2338
ISBN 0-13-695296-8
ISBN 0-13-695288-7 pbk.

Contents

Introduction

The secret for the success of the Prentice Hall Contract Bridge Series has been simple. Break down the science—and the fun—of bridge into its specialized elements, selecting those aspects of the game that will be of greatest help to the avid student and of greatest interest to the more experienced players. Then find the authors who are especially well-fitted to write about these elements clearly, authoritatively, entertainingly. Bob Ewen has been such a find.

When I suggested the idea of doing this book on Preemptive Bids to Bob, he was enthusiastic. Preemptives have always been big point-swingers—not always easy to use effectively and almost always difficult to compete against. Today's players are using preemptive bids far more often than ever before.

Ewen had already made two magnificent contributions to this series. His *"Opening Leads,"* published in 1970, speedily became the classic on this most important single play in the game. His 1973 book on *"Doubles"* amply justified my advice to all readers "to learn to wield the double-edge war ax so masterfully described." I think you will find what he has to say about preemptive bids equally clear, equally fascinating and equally helpful.

Bob Ewen's major field was—and perhaps still is —psychology, although the success of his bridge writings is one of the things that impelled him to abandon his former post as associate professor of psychology and assistant department chairman at New York University. Psychology is a most important element of bridge success and rarely is it applied more intensively than in the field of preemptive bids. Thus the present book is prepared to a surefire recipe:

Take a good writer and clear thinker—a star player who has already established his success both in playing bridge and writing about it. Turn him loose on a project that captures his enthusiasm and applies his college training. Result: a book that will provide both profit and entertainment to the reader and probably, as time will determine, another classic in its field.

If my editorship of this series had accomplished nothing else, I think it could stand on the claim of having launched Bob Ewen on what will no doubt continue to be an exceptionally successful bridge-writing career.

—Richard L. Frey

1

A Double-Edged Sword

♠ ♡ ◇ ♣

Preemptive bids create action, excitement, problems, and frequently disaster—for somebody. On the one hand, it's quite a thrill when your high-level opening bid or overcall turns almost certain defeat into victory. You may enjoy the fun of watching your unhappy opponents, crumbling visibly under the pressure, struggle into a 4-2 fit at the six-level (down three) when cold for a grand slam in a different suit, or carefully select their 4-2 trump fit (down two) when game would have been laydown in two other suits or in notrump. (Sound unlikely? These results actually happened in *expert* games, as we will see later on in this chapter.) Or your opponents may settle for a trivial penalty instead of racking up a much more lucrative game or slam. Life can be pretty grim, however, when you preempt and pay out 1100 or 1400 points for the privilege of preventing the opponents from making two clubs, or when partner properly passes your three-level preempt and later points out angrily that you were cold for slam in his suit.

Preemptive bids, then, are a double-edged sword; they may effectively cut down the opponents, but they may also turn against the user. And since Dame Fortune plays a considerable role in the outcome, there is no certain route to success. Some experts opt for boldness and preempt at the slightest excuse, accepting high risks in order to make the opponents' lives as difficult as possible. Others prefer to preempt only when they can do so with relative safety.

Our goal in this chapter is to survey the wide range of preempts currently in evidence among today's top players. One important caveat: The fact that a preempt succeeded does *not* necessarily mean that I recommend it. Similarly, a preempt that failed may actually have been a reasonable choice; responder may have taken an ill-advised course of action, or the opponents may have been very

1

lucky. A sampling of actual results is presented so that you can start to form some conclusions about the preemptive style that is right for you. And you'll also be prepared for whatever tactics you run into at the bridge table.

Preempts That Wrecked the Opponents

STANDARD PREEMPTS

A standard preemptive bid promises a long strong suit and very little side defensive strength. A common but rather conservative approach is to overbid by three tricks when not vulnerable and by two tricks when vulnerable. In the following deal, which arose in a Florida tournament, a single bid saved North and South well over 1000 points:

DEAL I
South dealer
East-West vulnerable

```
                    NORTH
                    ♠ Q J 7 5 2
                    ♡ A 10
                    ◇ J 6
                    ♣ K 10 8 5
WEST                                    EAST
♠ A 6                                   ♠ K 9 8 3
♡ 6 4 3 2                               ♡ —
◇ A K 7 3                               ◇ Q 10 8 5 4 2
♣ A Q 4                                 ♣ J 7 2
                    SOUTH
                    ♠ 10 4
                    ♡ K Q J 9 8 7 5
                    ◇ 9
                    ♣ 9 6 3
```

The bidding:

SOUTH	WEST	NORTH	EAST
3 ♡	Pass	Pass	Pass

Going down one didn't bother South at all, since the opponents were cold for slam. East and West, however, were highly dismayed to see their potential 1370-point bonanza turn into a meager 50-point profit.

"Couldn't you reopen?" grumbled West. "You had the heart void and the long suit, and it's easier for the player with good distribution to act over a preempt."

"If you think I should bid with this mess, you're crazy!" East retorted. "I'd be taking my life in my hands! I could easily go for 1100 when the opponents couldn't make anything at all, and I can imagine what you'd say about *that*. Besides, how many high-card points did *you* have? *Seventeen*?"

"I was stuck," West complained. "I couldn't bid notrump without a heart stopper, and I didn't have a suit worth a four-level overcall. And I could hardly double with such lousy spade support, for I'd really be up the creek if you happened to jump to 4 ♠."

"Well," muttered East, "I don't see how you can pass with so many points."

"And I don't understand how you could fail to protect me by passing with such fine distribution," West answered.

The argument waxed longer (and hotter), but South made no move to interrupt his expert opponents. He just leaned back in his chair and smiled. . . .

In our next deal, taken from the 1962 World Championships, a well-chosen preempt by the American West gave the U.S. one of its infrequent jackpots against the vaunted Italian Blue Team:

DEAL II
West dealer
Neither side vulnerable

NORTH
♠ A Q 10
♡ J 9 7 4
◇ A 6
♣ A 8 6 3

WEST
♠ 7 5
♡ Q
◇ 10 5
♣ K Q 10 9 7 5 4 2

EAST
♠ K J 9 4 2
♡ A K 10 6 5
◇ 9 3 2
♣ —

SOUTH
♠ 8 6 3
♡ 8 3 2
◇ K Q J 8 7 4
♣ J

When the U.S. held the East-West cards, West elected to open with 4 ♣. North doubled, East passed with an air of unconcern, and South jumped to 5 ◇. East doubled when this got around to him. The defenders collected two spade tricks, three heart tricks, and a club ruff—and 700 points.

When the deal was replayed, the Italian West decided to open with only 3 ♣. North doubled, East passed, and South wisely chose to bid just 3 ◇. Everyone passed. The Italian defenders also collected six tricks, but they wound up with a mere 100 points for their troubles.

The following deal is from a practice match involving the 1964 U.S. International Team. It is not clear that either North or South did anything terrible, but they had to pay out 800 points anyway.

DEAL III
East dealer
North-South vulnerable

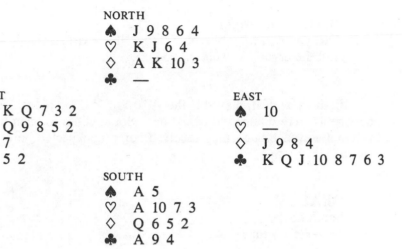

NORTH
♠ J 9 8 6 4
♡ K J 6 4
◇ A K 10 3
♣ —

WEST
♠ K Q 7 3 2
♡ Q 9 8 5 2
◇ 7
♣ 5 2

EAST
♠ 10
♡ —
◇ J 9 8 4
♣ K Q J 10 8 7 6 3

SOUTH
♠ A 5
♡ A 10 7 3
◇ Q 6 5 2
♣ A 9 4

East opened with 5 ♣, South doubled, West passed, and North cue-bid 6 ♣ to ask South to select his best side suit—a reasonable choice, but one that cost his side 1500 points! The eventual contract, 6 ♡ doubled, suffered a three-trick set; perfect defense would have brought home 700 points against 5 ♣ doubled.

Did South overbid? Or should North have passed the double despite his club void? North and South had *very* different opinions on that score.

"I had to double," South said. "I was sure that we were going to defeat 5 ♣, and I couldn't let them steal us blind!"

"I had to bid," North said. "It looked as though we'd beat 5 ♣ by only one or two tricks when we were cold for slam!"

"Let's settle this once and for all," South suggested. "We'll give my hand to a panel of experts and see what they decide."

And so they did, and the results were:

Pass: 7 votes
Double: 5 votes

"I win," said North.
"No you don't," objected South, "it's a virtual tie."
And the argument went on and on. . . .

In the next deal, played in the 1970 World Championships, the opponents were doomed to defeat once South chose to open with a preempt—even though they received some unexpected help from North.

DEAL IV
South dealer
East-West vulnerable

```
                        NORTH
                        ♠  J 10 6
                        ♡  A J 5
                        ◊  A J 10 4 2
                        ♣  10 3
WEST                                        EAST
♠  A K 9 7                                  ♠  8 4 3
♡  K 10 9 6                                 ♡  8 4 3
◊  K Q 9 7 5                                ◊  8 6 3
♣  —                                        ♣  A J 7 2
                        SOUTH
                        ♠  Q 5 2
                        ♡  Q 7 2
                        ◊  —
                        ♣  K Q 9 8 6 5 4
```

The bidding:

SOUTH	WEST	NORTH	EAST
China	U.S.	China	U.S.
3 ♣	Double	4 ♣	Double
Pass	Pass	Pass	

West had to act over South's 3 ♣ bid; but as luck would have it, his partner turned up with a horror. Had North just left well enough alone, East would have been faced with a delightful choice: He could pass and permit South to make 3 ♣ doubled, or he could bid one of his rather unimpressive suits and suffer a sizeable penalty. North, however, came to the rescue of his hapless opponents by inserting an uninspired raise to 4 ♣. Then East promptly got his side back into trouble by doubling for penalties. So the preempt worked well after all. South played East for the missing trumps and finessed the ten of clubs at once, eventually took the heart finesse and discarded his losing heart on the ace of diamonds, and wound up losing only the trump ace and two spade tricks. When the deal was replayed in the other room, the American South elected to pass, and East-West never got into trouble.

In the following deal, which occurred in a match between Brazil and Venezuela during the 1971 South American Championships, it isn't all that easy for North and South to reach their only makable game even if the opponents leave them strictly alone. After an enemy preempt, however, it's virtually impossible.

DEAL V
East dealer
Both sides vulnerable

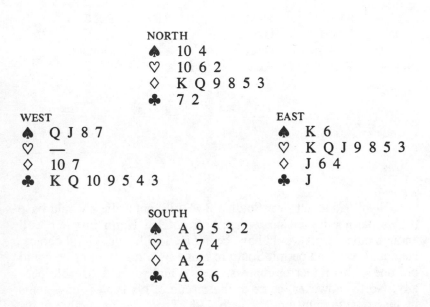

East opened with a preempt of 3 ♡, and South, who probably entertained some serious thoughts about switching to gin rummy, chose to double. West passed, North bid 4 ◇, and South corrected (?) to 4 ♠—down four. Instead of quickly wrapping up nine tricks in notrump, North and South had to pay a penalty of 400 points.

Sometimes a preempt causes the opponents to go completely haywire. Here's one of the 4-2 fits promised earlier, which won an important tournament team match for East and West:

DEAL VI
East dealer
North-South vulnerable

```
                        NORTH
                        ♠  K J
                        ♡  K 9 7 6 4
                        ◇  A Q
                        ♣  K 7 4 3
WEST                                        EAST
♠  10 7 6 5 3                               ♠  9 4
♡  J                                        ♡  A Q 10 8 5 3 2
◇  J 9 2                                    ◇  5
♣  J 10 9 8                                 ♣  Q 6 2
                        SOUTH
                        ♠  A Q 8 2
                        ♡  —
                        ◇  K 10 8 7 6 4 3
                        ♣  A 5
```

Although East didn't know it, his teammates in the other room had reached only 6 ◇ with the North-South cards. This would have meant ultimate defeat if North-South now bid the grand slam, but preemptive bidding turned this dire situation into a surprising victory. East opened with 3 ♡, and South, who was using an overcall in the cheapest unbid minor suit as a request to partner to take out to his best suit, decided to eschew his powerful diamonds and bid 4 ♣. North leaped directly to 6 ♣, and South went into a long huddle. Eventually he talked himself into the notion that North had a long and solid club suit, so he *passed*.

Down three, and 300 points—and the match—to a delighted East-West!

PREEMPTS IN THIRD POSITION

When partner has passed originally, it is customary to modify the requirements for a preemptive opening bid. Since his silence makes slam unlikely, one common ploy is to preempt with an unusually strong hand and make the opponents guess what to do:

DEAL VII
West dealer
Both sides vulnerable

```
                        NORTH
                        ♠  10 8 7
                        ♡  Q 2
                        ◇  J 9 8 6
                        ♣  8 6 3 2
WEST                                         EAST
♠  9 5 3 2                                   ♠  6
♡  10 3                                      ♡  A K J 9 8 7 5
◇  K 7 3 2                                   ◇  5 4
♣  J 10 5                                    ♣  A Q 7
                        SOUTH
                        ♠  A K Q J 4
                        ♡  6 4
                        ◇  A Q 10
                        ♣  K 9 4
```

In first or second position, the East hand should be opened with 1 ♡; the appreciable defensive strength in clubs renders the hand too powerful for a preempt. When this deal arose in the 1971 World Championships, however, West dealt and passed and North also passed. Both the American and French Easts chose to open with 4 ♡. The French South guessed wrong: He doubled, could not defeat the contract, and shelled out 790 points. The American South, however, overcalled with 4 ♠, escaped for down one undoubled, and paid only 100 points.

Another common strategy when in third position is to preempt with a weaker suit than usual. Here's an example from the 1970 World Championships:

DEAL VIII
West dealer
North-South vulnerable

NORTH (Brazil)
♠ A Q 10
♡ A 9 8 7
◇ 9 4
♣ J 9 8 6

WEST (U.S.)
♠ 9 5 2
♡ K J 10 5 2
◇ 10 5 3
♣ Q 10

EAST (U.S.)
♠ J 4 3
♡ 6 4
◇ Q 6
♣ A K 7 4 3 2

SOUTH (Brazil)
♠ K 8 7 6
♡ Q 3
◇ A K J 8 7 2
♣ 5

West dealt and passed, and North also passed. A pass by East could not be criticized, but he realized that South was undoubtedly holding a goodly number of the outstanding high cards. To make the task of his vulnerable opponents as rough as possible, East elected to open with 3 ♣ in spite of his shaky suit. South overcalled with 3 ◇, West risked a doubtful raise to 4 ♣, North bid 4 ♡, and everyone passed! Game in diamonds, spades, or notrump is there for the taking as the cards lie; but the ill-conceived heart contract had no chance, and North went down two. It turned out that quite a bit was at stake, for the American North and South players in the other room took a conservative course and stopped in a 3 ◇ partial.

PREEMPTIVE OVERCALLS

Preemptive overcalls are essentially similar to preemptive opening bids. Here's an example from the Trials to select the 1971 U.S. International Team:

DEAL IX
North dealer
East-West vulnerable

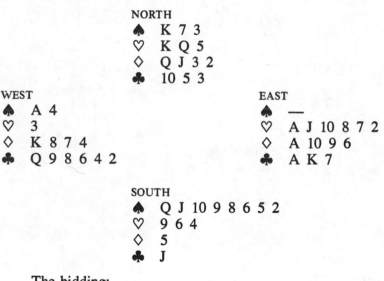

NORTH
♠ K 7 3
♡ K Q 5
◇ Q J 3 2
♣ 10 5 3

WEST
♠ A 4
♡ 3
◇ K 8 7 4
♣ Q 9 8 6 4 2

EAST
♠ —
♡ A J 10 8 7 2
◇ A 10 9 6
♣ A K 7

SOUTH
♠ Q J 10 9 8 6 5 2
♡ 9 6 4
◇ 5
♣ J

The bidding:

SOUTH	WEST	NORTH	EAST
—	—	Pass	1 ♡
4 ♠	Double	Pass	Pass
Pass			

South decided to shade his preempt somewhat and overbid by four tricks because of his partner's initial pass, and he was very happy with the result. West, fearing a disastrous misfit, decided not to mention his clubs. East, concluding that his partner was loaded with trumps, saw no reason to bid again. The outcome was that East-West wound up with a 300-point penalty—and about 1000 points less than the club slam that was there for the taking.

In the following deal from the 1962 World Championships, a member of the Italian Blue Team preempted despite a strong no-trump opening bid on his right, and produced a result that a certain U.S. pair would *very* much like to forget!

DEAL X
East dealer
Neither side vulnerable

```
                        NORTH
                        ♠  —
                        ♡  K 10 5 3
                        ◇  Q 9 8 6
                        ♣  A K J 8 7
WEST                                        EAST
♠  A Q 10 9 8 7 4 3                         ♠  6 5 2
♡  4                                        ♡  A J 8 6 2
◇  —                                        ◇  7 5 3
♣  10 9 6 4                                 ♣  5 2
                        SOUTH
                        ♠  K J
                        ♡  Q 9 7
                        ◇  A K J 10 4 2
                        ♣  Q 3
```

The bidding:

SOUTH	WEST	NORTH	EAST
U.S.	Italy	U.S.	Italy
—	—	—	Pass
1 NT	3 ♠	4 ♠	Pass
4 NT	Pass	Pass	Pass

When this deal was played in the other room, the American East-West players quite properly sacrificed in 6 ♠ doubled against the icy diamond slam. Here, however, the auction took a surprising turn, and the Italian West exploited his advantage to the full by leading his small heart. East hopped up with the ace and fired back a spade through declarer's king, and West happily ran off an immense number of spade tricks.

Down *six*. And, for the U.S., the dubious distinction of finding one of the few ways of achieving a minus score with the North-South cards!

UNUSUAL PREEMPTS

Since high-level opening bids and overcalls can cause the opponents so much trouble, some players relax (or perhaps even abandon) the requirements for making a preemptive bid. Sometimes this involves nothing more than opening one trick light:

DEAL XI
West dealer
North-South vulnerable

```
                        NORTH
                        ♠  Q J 10 7 6 2
                        ♡  A Q 8 6 5
                        ◇  —
                        ♣  J 7
WEST                                          EAST
♠  8 5                                        ♠  4 3
♡  7 3                                        ♡  J 10 9 2
◇  10 9 2                                     ◇  J 7 6 3
♣  K Q 10 9 8 5                               ♣  A 4 2
                        SOUTH
                        ♠  A K 9
                        ♡  K 4
                        ◇  A K Q 8 5 4
                        ♣  6 3
```

The bidding, Room 1:

SOUTH	WEST	NORTH	EAST
U.S.	Norway	U.S.	Norway
—	3 ♣	3 ♠	5 ♣
6 ♣	Pass	6 ♠	Pass
Pass	Pass		

The bidding, Room 2:

SOUTH	WEST	NORTH	EAST
Norway	U.S.	Norway	U.S.
—	3 ♣	4 ♣	5 ♣
7 ♦	Pass	Pass	Pass

Strict adherence to traditional conservative guidelines would require a pass with the West cards, since six tricks are needed for a non-vulnerable three-level preempt. However, few modern experts are that rigid. When this deal was played in the 1970 World Championships, the West players at both tables elected to open with 3 ♣ in an attempt to sabotage their vulnerable opponents, and the results were little short of spectacular. The American North-South, refusing to be intimidated, cranked their bidding machinery into high gear and proceeded directly to 6 ♠, down one. But Norway fared even worse. They careened into 7 ♦ with the North-South cards and went down three, so the U.S. actually gained 200 points on the deal.

In our next example, which arose in the Trials to select the 1969 U.S. International Team, East had to bend the rules even more in order to open with a preempt. His partner, however, did not utter a word of complaint—no doubt because East succeeded in talking his world-famous opponents out of a grand slam.

DEAL XII
North dealer
North-South vulnerable

```
                        NORTH
                        ♠   7 5
                        ♡   K J 7 5
                        ◇   K J 6
                        ♣   Q 7 5 4
WEST                                            EAST
♠   Q 6                                         ♠   J 10 9 8 4 2
♡   10 8 6 4 2                                  ♡   9
◇   8 5 4 2                                     ◇   3
♣   10 3                                        ♣   K J 9 6 2
                        SOUTH
                        ♠   A K 3
                        ♡   A Q 3
                        ◇   A Q 10 9 7
                        ♣   A 8
```

The bidding:

SOUTH	WEST	NORTH	EAST
—	—	Pass	3 ♠
3 NT	Pass	Pass	Pass

Opening a doubtful preempt in *second* seat is a risky proposition. One opponent has already announced weakness by passing and partner has not yet been heard from, so your side may well own the balance of power and the preempt may succeed only in derailing your own bidding. This time, however, East was in luck for South had the powerhouse—and no good way to describe it once the preempt forced him to begin operations at the three-level. A double or a diamond overcall didn't seem quite right, so South tried 3 NT. North, allowing for the fact that South might be stretching with a markedly weaker hand in order to avoid being shut out, elected to pass. And making game was a victory of Pyrrhic proportions, for grand slam was icy in diamonds or (as the cards lie) even in notrump.*

Many players refuse to preempt when they hold a side four-card or longer *major* suit, for fear of shutting themselves out of their own best contract. In the following deal, however, North chose to violate this rule:

---

*South cashes the club ace, runs five diamonds and pitches two low clubs from dummy, and cashes four hearts (discarding a club from his hand). East is squeezed in the black suits.

DEAL XIII
South dealer
Both sides vulnerable

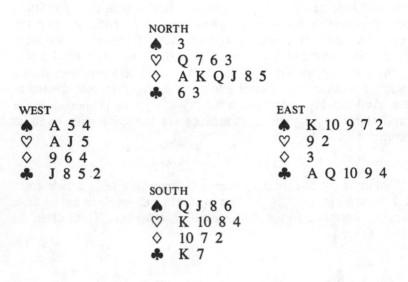

NORTH
♠ 3
♡ Q 7 6 3
◇ A K Q J 8 5
♣ 6 3

WEST
♠ A 5 4
♡ A J 5
◇ 9 6 4
♣ J 8 5 2

EAST
♠ K 10 9 7 2
♡ 9 2
◇ 3
♣ A Q 10 9 4

SOUTH
♠ Q J 8 6
♡ K 10 8 4
◇ 10 7 2
♣ K 7

The bidding:

SOUTH	WEST	NORTH	EAST
Pass	Pass	3 ◇	3 ♠
Pass	4 ♠	Pass	Pass
Pass			

This deal occurred during the playoffs to select the 1973 U.S. International Team. North's opening bid was unusual even for a third-position preempt, for it might well have talked his own side out of game in hearts or notrump. The actual result, however, was a modest gain. East felt obliged to overbid slightly with his fine distributional hand in order to contest the issue before it was too late. And West, speculating that his partner might have a very strong hand, also decided on an aggressive course of action and bid one more for game. The combined East-West assets proved too meager to sustain a four-level contract, and East eventually went down two.

In the 1963 World Championships, a member of the Italian Blue Team also turned disdain for the heart suit into a handsome profit:

DEAL XIV
East dealer
Neither side vulnerable

```
                        NORTH
                        ♠  J 6 4
                        ♡  A K Q 10 8
                        ◇  10
                        ♣  K 8 6 3
WEST                                         EAST
♠  K 10 8 7 5 3                              ♠  2
♡  J 7                                       ♡  9 6 5 3 2
◇  8 6 5                                     ◇  A K Q J 9 4
♣  J 7                                       ♣  4
                        SOUTH
                        ♠  A Q 9
                        ♡  4
                        ◇  7 3 2
                        ♣  A Q 10 9 5 2
```

The bidding:

SOUTH U.S.	WEST Italy	NORTH U.S.	EAST Italy
—	—	—	3 ◇
Pass	Pass	3 ♡	Pass
4 ♣	Pass	5 ♣	Pass
Pass	Pass		

The Americans stopped too low, while the Italians bid and made 6 ♣ in the other room. Some analysts indicted South for excessive underbidding, while others attributed the blame primarily to East's unorthodox preempt. East was delighted to own up to his share of the responsibility, but South is still arguing about what would have happened if West had turned up with five clubs to the king, jack, and. . . .

The Americans may have hoped for a respite when the Blue Team declined to play in the 1970 World Championships, but the substitute Italian squad proved equally adept at creating preemptive predicaments:

DEAL XV
West dealer
Neither side vulnerable

```
                         NORTH
                         ♠  K
                         ♡  8 6 3
                         ◇  K
                         ♣  K Q J 10 9 8 7 2
     WEST                                      EAST
     ♠  A 10 8 6 4 2                           ♠  J 7 3
     ♡  10 9 4                                 ♡  A K 5 2
     ◇  Q J 8 7                                ◇  9 5 3 2
     ♣  —                                      ♣  6 4
                         SOUTH
                         ♠  Q 9 5
                         ♡  Q J 7
                         ◇  A 10 6 4
                         ♣  A 5 3
```

The bidding, Room 1:

SOUTH	WEST	NORTH	EAST
U.S.	Italy	U.S.	Italy
—	3 ♠	4 ♣	4 ♠
5 ♣	Pass	Pass	Pass

The bidding, Room 2:

SOUTH	WEST	NORTH	EAST
Italy	U.S.	Italy	U.S.
—	Pass	Pass	Pass
1 ◇	1 ♠	2 ♠	Pass
2 NT	Pass	3 ♣	Pass
3 NT	Pass	Pass	Pass

The Italian West *did* preempt despite his atypical distribution, and succeeded in pushing the American North-South into an unmakable contract. The Italian North, however, *did not* preempt despite his superb club suit, and was rewarded when his side was able to reach the laydown game in notrump. (Fortunately, this unfriendly result did not prevent the U.S. from bringing home their first World Championship in sixteen years.)

The next deal, which occurred during the 1969 U.S. Spring National Team of Four Championships, illustrates the lengths to which some players will go in order to preempt when the opponents are vulnerable and they are not. If such flights of fancy succeed, analysts refer to them with terms like "artful bidding barrage." If they fail, they are apt to be described as "lunatic preempts." Take a look at this artful bidding barrage:

DEAL XVI
West dealer
North-South vulnerable

```
                        NORTH
                        ♠ A 9 6 3 2
                        ♡ Q J 9 6
                        ◇ Q 9
                        ♣ A Q
WEST                                              EAST
♠ 10 8 7 4                                        ♠ J 5
♡ —                                               ♡ A K 10 8 7
◇ 10 8 2                                          ◇ A K 7 4 3
♣ K 10 9 6 4 3                                    ♣ 7
                        SOUTH
                        ♠ K Q
                        ♡ 5 4 3 2
                        ◇ J 6 5
                        ♣ J 8 5 2
```

The bidding:

SOUTH	WEST	NORTH	EAST
—	3 ♣	Double	Pass
3 ♡	Pass	4 ♡	Double
Pass	Pass	Pass	

South had a gruesome time playing 4 ♡ doubled, and eventually went for 1100. When the deal was replayed in the other room, West started off with a normal pass. North was able to learn about South's weakness in time and let the opponents buy the hand for 3 ◇, registering a one-trick set.

Here's another extreme example, this time from the 1969 World Championships:

DEAL XVII
West dealer
North-South vulnerable

```
                        NORTH
                        ♠  Q 8 6 5 4
                        ♡  A K 8 7 5 3
                        ◊  10 4
                        ♣  —
WEST                                          EAST
♠  K 7 2                                      ♠  J 9 3
♡  Q 9                                        ♡  6 4
◊  K 9 8 5                                    ◊  Q 2
♣  Q 8 6 4                                    ♣  A 10 9 7 3 2
                        SOUTH
                        ♠  A 10
                        ♡  J 10 2
                        ◊  A J 7 6 3
                        ♣  K J 5
```

The bidding:

SOUTH	WEST	NORTH	EAST
Brazil	U.S.	Brazil	U.S.
—	Pass	Pass	3 ♣
Pass	4 ♣	Double	Pass
5 ◊	Pass	Pass	Pass

Game in hearts would have been easy but 5 ◊ had no chance, and South went down three. Who was the culprit? When this hand was submitted to a panel of experts for adjudication, every one of the North-South actions came under fire. A few experts would have opened the bidding with North's hand, and some would have made a direct overcall with South's cards. Some argued that North should have bid 4 ♡ instead of doubling; some claimed that *South* should have bid 4 ♡ rather than 5 ◊; others decided that South should have passed the double and settled for a sure plus score. Presumably, North and South are still arguing. . . .

If you think that the last two preempts were wild, take a look at this exhibit from the playoff to determine the 1971 U.S. International Team:

DEAL XVIII
East dealer
North-South vulnerable

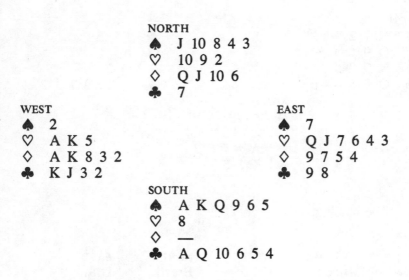

NORTH
♠ J 10 8 4 3
♡ 10 9 2
♢ Q J 10 6
♣ 7

WEST
♠ 2
♡ A K 5
♢ A K 8 3 2
♣ K J 3 2

EAST
♠ 7
♡ Q J 7 6 4 3
♢ 9 7 5 4
♣ 9 8

SOUTH
♠ A K Q 9 6 5
♡ 8
♢ —
♣ A Q 10 6 5 4

The bidding:

SOUTH	WEST	NORTH	EAST
—	—	—	3 ♡
Double	4 ♡	Pass	Pass
4 ♠	Double	Pass	Pass
Pass			

Obviously, East was *rather* determined to disrupt the auction of his vulnerable opponents. South opted to bid slowly in the hope of luring a double from an unwary West, easily took twelve tricks, and scored up 1190 points—and a net *loss* of 470 points on the deal!

In the other room East chose to pass, and North and South bid quickly and easily to 6 ♠. West doubled (would *you* have sacrificed in 7 ♡?), sighed when his ace of diamonds was ruffed, cried when his club tricks disappeared, and paid out 1660 points.

The following preempt, which also occurred during the Trials to select the 1971 U.S. International Team, was even more bizarre—and even more profitable:

DEAL XIX
West dealer
North-South vulnerable

```
                      NORTH
                      ♠  A K
                      ♡  K J 9 8 3
                      ◇  A Q 9 8 3
                      ♣  K
WEST                                         EAST
♠  J 10 9 8 3 2                              ♠  7 5 4
♡  10 7                                      ♡  A 6
◇  5                                         ◇  J 10 4 2
♣  8 7 4 3                                   ♣  A Q 9 5
                      SOUTH
                      ♠  Q 6
                      ♡  Q 5 4 2
                      ◇  K 7 6
                      ♣  J 10 6 2
```

The bidding:

SOUTH	WEST	NORTH	EAST
—	3 ♠	Double	4 ♠
Double	Pass	5 ♠	Pass
6 ♡	Pass	Pass	Double
Pass	Pass	Pass	

South's attempt to take twelve tricks missing two cashable aces was not notably successful, and he went down one.

Cast an eye at this deal from an expert (?) rubber bridge game:

DEAL XX
East dealer
North-South vulnerable

```
                        NORTH
                        ♠  A Q 10 7 6 4
                        ♡  A 9 3
                        ◊  K 5
                        ♣  A 3
        WEST                                    EAST
        ♠  J 9 8                                ♠  3 2
        ♡  K 8                                  ♡  J 7 5 4
        ◊  J 10 8 3 2                           ◊  9
        ♣  5 4 2                                ♣  J 10 9 8 7 6
                        SOUTH
                        ♠  K 5
                        ♡  Q 10 6 2
                        ◊  A Q 7 6 4
                        ♣  K Q
```

The bidding:

SOUTH	WEST	NORTH	EAST
—	—	—	3 ♣
3 ◊	4 ♣	5 ♣	Pass
5 ◊	Pass	7 ◊	Pass
Pass	Pass		

North-South reached a hopeless contract when a lucrative small slam in spades or notrump was there for the taking. Their "discussion" about this quaint result lasted *quite* a while. . . .

As you can see, preemptive bids can be devastating weapons even against expert opponents. But before you get carried away and start preempting with five-card suits headed by the eight-spot, let's take a look at the other side of this potent but double-edged sword.

Preempts That Wrecked the Preempter

Several (large) books would be needed in order to present the many deals wherein a preempt based on an awful suit went for 1400 while the opponents, if left to their own devices, might perhaps have made one heart with the aid of a couple of defensive errors. A few celebrated cases are worth noting, however:

♠ K 6
♡ Q 4 2
◇ K 7 6 4 3 2
♣ J 7

A renowned U.S. player held these cards in the 1958 World Championships—and soon wished that he had never seen any of them! The Blue Team player on his left opened with 1 ♣, an artificial bid promising at least 17 points. His partner passed, and his right-hand opponent bid 2 ♣, a conventional call showing either an ace and a king or three kings. *"Three diamonds,"* chirped our hero, undaunted by the vast number of high cards known to be located with the enemy.

Down *seven*, doubled. And so the Americans earned the privilege of paying out 1300 points to stop their opponents from recording a 600-point game.

Here's another North American World Championship disaster; it took place in 1967. This time the preempter had an excuse, for he was behind in the match and was trying to generate a swing. He got one—but not the kind he wanted.

♠ 8 2
♡ K 10
◇ 8 6 4
♣ Q J 10 8 3 2

Not vulnerable against vulnerable opponents, he chose to open with 3 ♣. The next two players passed, and the Blue Team opponent on his right reopened with a double. His left-hand opponent, looking at no fewer than *six* clubs, was delighted to pass. His partner, expecting a healthier suit for the three-level preempt, failed to find the successful escape to 3 ◇. The bill ultimately came to 900 points, a net loss of 250 since the Americans in the other room could score only 650 by making their game contract.

Strategic third-position preempts can also backfire:

♠ A 6
♡ K Q 10 8 7 6 2
◇ K 3
♣ Q 5

After two passes, the player who held this hand in the 1971 European Championships elected to open with 4 ♡ and "make the opponents guess." They promptly doubled, his partner turned up with a singleton heart and one king on the side, and he shelled out 700 points. A normal 1 ♡ opening bid would have unearthed partner's weakness in time—and limited the loss to approximately 100 points.

In addition to producing catastrophic penalties, there are some inventive and unusual ways in which preemptive bids can destroy the preempter:

DEAL XXI
South dealer
Both sides vulnerable

```
                    NORTH
                    ♠  2
                    ♡  A Q 10 5 4 3
                    ◇  A K J 10 9
                    ♣  5
WEST                                        EAST
♠  A 9 6 5 3                                ♠  K Q J 4
♡  7 6 2                                    ♡  K J 9 8
◇  7 5                                      ◇  Q 6
♣  7 4 3                                    ♣  A 10 2
                    SOUTH
                    ♠  10 8 7
                    ♡  —
                    ◇  8 4 3 2
                    ♣  K Q J 9 8 6
```

The bidding:

SOUTH	WEST	NORTH	EAST
U.S.	Britain	U.S.	Britain
3 ♣	Pass	3 ♡	Double
4 ♣	Pass	Pass	Pass

Preempting with a hand like South's can prevent locating a good contract in one of the other suits, and so it proved when this deal was played in the 1962 World Championships. A trump lead and a spade shift defeats 4 ♣, while game in diamonds is there for the taking—and was duly reached by the British North-South in the other room.

A preempt can also backfire by guiding declarer to the only winning line of play. Here's an interesting example from a 1957 National Tournament:

DEAL XXII
North dealer
Both sides vulnerable

```
                      NORTH
                      ♠  J 7 6
                      ♡  Q 10 9 7
                      ◇  A 7 5
                      ♣  K Q 10
WEST                                      EAST
♠  K                                      ♠  10 5 4 2
♡  6 5 3                                  ♡  —
◇  3 2                                    ◇  K Q J 10 9 8 6
♣  9 8 7 6 4 3 2                          ♣  A 5
                      SOUTH
                      ♠  A Q 9 8 3
                      ♡  A K J 8 4 2
                      ◇  4
                      ♣  J
```

The bidding:

SOUTH	WEST	NORTH	EAST
—	—	Pass	4 ◊
4 ♡	Pass	5 ◊	Pass
5 ♠	Pass	6 ♡	Pass
Pass	Pass		

West led the three of diamonds, and North's ace won the trick. The slam hinged on picking up the spade suit, so South set out to get as much information as possible. He ruffed a diamond with the ace of hearts and drew three rounds of trumps, ending in dummy. He then ruffed another diamond in his hand, noting West's discard of a small club, and played the jack of clubs. East won with the ace and returned a club. South cashed dummy's high clubs, pitching a couple of low spades.

When East discarded on the third round of clubs, his distribution was crystal clear. West was known to have begun with exactly two diamonds, so East was marked with a seven-card suit. Since East had turned up with two clubs and no hearts at all, his remaining four cards could only be spades.

Ordinarily, South would now play East for four spades to the king-ten and take two finesses—and go down. Here, however, is where East's preempt gave the show away: With seven superb diamonds and an ace *and a king* on the side, he surely would have opened with 1 ◊. Therefore South (Ivar Stakgold) disdained the finesse and laid down the ace of spades to bring home his difficult slam contract.

Watching the opponents happily chalk up a small slam because of the information provided by the preempt is bad enough, but the next deal—from the Trials to select the 1973 U.S. International Team —proved to be even worse:

DEAL XXIII
West dealer
East-West vulnerable

NORTH
♠ Q J 4 3
♡ A K Q 6 2
♢ 6
♣ A 7 2

WEST
♠ —
♡ 7 3
♢ J 10 7 5 2
♣ K Q J 10 9 8

EAST
♠ 10 7 6 2
♡ J
♢ K Q 9 8 3
♣ 6 5 3

SOUTH
♠ A K 9 8 5
♡ 10 9 8 5 4
♢ A 4
♣ 4

The bidding:

SOUTH	WEST	NORTH	EAST
—	3 ♣	Double	Pass
4 ♣	Pass	5 ♣	Pass
7 ♠	Pass	Pass	Pass

South's 4 ♣ cue-bid said, "I've got a strong hand, how about picking the suit?" And North's 5 ♣ bid answered, "No, *you* pick the suit." He realized that West, who was marked with a lot of clubs because of his preempt, might well be void in a side suit; and so, to prevent a disastrous ruff at trick one, it was desirable for South to play the hand. This fine display of teamwork was well rewarded, for the resulting grand slam could not be defeated.

When the deal was replayed in the other room, West discreetly passed at his first turn; and, with no warning to guide them, his opponents landed in 7 ♡ played by *North*. East found the spade lead to set the contract one trick. The huge gain on this deal helped the recipients win the Trials and reach the 1973 World Championships.

Sometimes a preempt achieves the dubious distinction of pushing the opponents into a top contract that they never would have reached on their own. In the following deal, played in the 1964 World Championships, the U.S. gained a measure of revenge against the British for the setback on Deal 21:

DEAL XXIV
West dealer
North-South vulnerable

```
                       NORTH
                       ♠  J 8 2
                       ♡  K Q 5 4
                       ◇  K
                       ♣  Q J 8 7 6
WEST                                         EAST
♠  K 10 9 7 6 4 3                            ♠  —
♡  8                                         ♡  10 7 6 2
◇  4 2                                       ◇  A 10 9 8 7 3
♣  K 10 2                                    ♣  A 9 3
                       SOUTH
                       ♠  A Q 5
                       ♡  A J 9 3
                       ◇  Q J 6 5
                       ♣  5 4
```

The bidding:

SOUTH	WEST	NORTH	EAST
U.S.	Britain	U.S.	Britain
—	3 ♠	Pass	Pass
3 NT	Pass	Pass	Pass

Left to their own devices, North-South probably would have reached 4 ♡ and gone down. After the preempt, however, South took a flier and landed on his feet. The defenders could not possibly set up and cash either of their long suits, so South wound up with two spade tricks, four hearts, two diamonds, and a club—and his game contract. Kenneth Konstam, the British internationalist who held the West cards, described his feelings this way in the June 1964 *Bridge World:* " . . . by no stretch of the imagination could South be considered to have his bid, but an old theory of mine was once again proved right: An opening three-bid is a mixed blessing. It often galvanizes the opponents into action they would never otherwise take. . . ."

Our next deal also supports the point that if you aren't lucky, you might as well stay in bed. It occurred during the Trials to select the 1965 U.S. International Team:

DEAL XXV
East dealer
North-South vulnerable

```
                    NORTH
                    ♠  A J 10 8 5
                    ♡  A Q 6 4
                    ◇  A Q 3
                    ♣  A
WEST                                    EAST
♠  K 9 2                                ♠  Q 3
♡  K 8                                  ♡  10 9 3
◇  10 9 8 5                             ◇  J 2
♣  J 10 9 7                             ♣  K Q 6 4 3 2
                    SOUTH
                    ♠  7 6 4
                    ♡  J 7 5 2
                    ◇  K 7 6 4
                    ♣  8 5
```

The bidding:

SOUTH	WEST	NORTH	EAST
—	—	—	3 ♣
Pass	5 ♣	6 ♣	Pass
6 ♡	Pass	Pass	Pass

East opted to confound his vulnerable opponents by making a light non-vulnerable preempt; and, with the aid of his partner, he succeeded in pushing them into a horrible contract. But look what happened during the play: South won the club lead with dummy's ace, led a small diamond to his king, and played a small heart, finessing North's queen. When it won, he sighed with relief, uncrossed his fingers, crossed his toes, and played the ace of hearts. When the king came tumbling down, the probable trump loser disappeared. The spade situation was still ominous, however, for South lacked the entries to take two finesses; but Lady Luck was not about to abandon him at this point. South played the *jack of spades* from dummy, and the defenders expired. If East ducked, his honor could be captured by dummy's ace on the next round of spades; and when he actually won with the queen, South entered his hand in hearts and took the finesse against West's king of spades to bring home his remarkable slam.

I haven't calculated the odds of finding a doubleton king of hearts in the West hand and picking up the spades with only one loser; but I do know that if I bounced the opponents into a contract like this only to see them make it, I'd give up bridge for a month.

Well, at least for a week.

2

The Art of Being Difficult

♠ ♡ ◇ ♣

Now that we have seen how devastating preemptive bids can be, let's tackle the question of when and how to use these bidding weapons.

Preemptive Opening Bids

A preemptive opening bid promises a long, strong suit and denies much outside defensive strength; one ace or king in the side suits is usually the limit. For example, these hands are excellent for preemptive purposes:

(a)
♠ K Q J 10 9 7 5 2
♡ 5 4
◇ 6 2
♣ 5

(b)
♠ A 4
♡ 8 6 5
◇ Q J 10 9 7 5 2
♣ 3

You have every right to insist that the hand be played in your suit in the event that your side buys the contract; and you very much want to make life as difficult as possible for your opponents, since they may well hold the balance of power and be hoping to exchange a lot of information at low levels of bidding. A preemptive opening bid is therefore ideal, for it will accomplish both objectives.

The following hands, however, should *not* normally be opened with a preempt:

37

(c) ♠ 9 8 7 6 5 3 2   (d) ♠ A 6 3
     ♥ A 6 5   ♥ A Q J 10 7 6 2
     ♦ A 7   ♦ Q 4
     ♣ J   ♣ 6

Hand (c) has excellent defensive strength and a terrible suit —exactly the opposite of a good preempt. A high-level opening bid may cause partner to take an eventual sacrifice against the opponents' game or slam, only to find that their contract would have easily been defeated because of your unexpected high cards. Or he may properly allow you to play in your suit, down several, when you could have registered a good plus score in his suit *if* you had given him a decent chance to bid it. Therefore your best procedure with this hand will usually be to pass.

Hand (d) has too much all-around strength for a preempt in first or second position. It meets all the requirements for a one-level opening, so you should definitely bid 1 ♥.

When you do preempt, how high should you bid? In the earlier days of bridge, most players followed the "Rule of Two and Three"; they overbid by three tricks when not vulnerable and by two tricks when vulnerable. For example, hand (a) will take seven tricks, so they would open 4 ♠ if not vulnerable and 3 ♠ if vulnerable. With hand (b), which is worth six tricks, they would bid 3 ♦ if not vulnerable and pass if vulnerable. Today's knowledgeable bridge player, however, is markedly more aggressive than this. (For example, you shouldn't dream of passing with hand (b) even if you happen to be vulnerable.) There are two main reasons for this important modern trend:

1. The level of skill is much higher today than it was ten or fifteen years ago. Therefore there is a great chance that the opponents, if left alone, will get to a decent contract; consequently, there is more to be gained by trying to preempt them into a state of confusion.

2. The double has undergone a change in meaning. No longer is it used solely (or even primarily) to increase a prospective penalty. Instead, many experts use the double of a preemptive opening bid or overcall to suggest, or even to require, that partner take out to his best suit. These modern doubles do not by any means rule out

the possibility of collecting a substantial penalty, but they let potentially catastrophic bids escape unpunished somewhat more often. As a result, preempting is not quite as risky as it used to be.

In most situations, therefore, the Rule of Two and Three is a thing of the past. The modern approach is to base preemptive decisions on several important factors, namely:

1. The vulnerability.
2. Your position at the table.
3. Your opponents' skill.
4. Your opponents' bidding methods.
5. The form of scoring.
6. The "state of the match."
7. The presence or absence of exceptional holdings.

We will consider each of these in turn.

THE VULNERABILITY

The vulnerability has an extremely strong effect on your potential preempt. To see why, let's suppose that you are playing in a "Swiss" or knockout team match, where every deal is scored separately, and see what might happen under each of the four conditions of vulnerability:*

1. You are not vulnerable and the opponents are (favorable vulnerability). This is the best time to preempt, for any enemy game or slam is worth relatively more and any penalty that you might suffer is worth relatively less. For example, suppose that the opponents double and set you two tricks instead of bidding and making their game. You pay out 300 points instead of 600, and save yourself a cool 300 points. And even if partner turns up with a real horror (enough defensive strength to stop the opponents from making a

---

*For simplicity, we will assume that the opponents can make 3 NT with no overtricks, which is worth 400 points not vulnerable (100 for the trick score and 300 for the game bonus) and 600 points vulnerable (100 for the trick score and 500 for the game bonus). In rubber bridge the bonuses are slightly different; the general argument still applies but with some exceptions, as we will see later in this chapter.

slam, but not enough high cards to help you take any tricks) and you go down four, the world will not have ended. True, you will incur a 700-point penalty, but that's only 100 points more than the opponents would have made had you left them alone.

2. Neither side is vulnerable. This is not as favorable a situation for preemption as the preceding case, for the opponents' game or slam is worth less. A two-trick set, doubled, will gain you only 100 points as opposed to letting them bid and make game, for you will pay a 300-point penalty instead of giving up 400. And going down four will blow 300 points, for you must shell out 700 when you could have gotten out for 400.

3. Both sides are vulnerable. This is slightly less auspicious than the preceding situation, for your potential penalty escalates faster than the increase in value of the enemy game or slam. Thus, going down two, doubled, will still save you 100 points compared to letting them bid and make their game, for you will lose 500 instead of 600. But if things go badly and you wind up down four, you'll have thrown away no fewer than 500 points by paying out 1100 instead of 600.

4. Only your side is vulnerable (unfavorable vulnerability). This is clearly the worst time to preempt. Even going down two, doubled, costs more than the opponents' game, for you lose 500 instead of 400. And down four is an absolute catastrophe that may have you shopping around for a new partner, for the 1100-point penalty will hand your delighted opponents 700 points more than they would have made on their own.

Since we have had to contend with a lot of numbers in this section, let's summarize the various outcomes in terms of net gain or loss:

The opponents have game but not slam, and they double and set you:

Vulnerability	*Two*	*Four*
Favorable (opponents only)	Gain 300	Lose 100
Neither side	Gain 100	Lose 300
Both sides	Gain 100	Lose 500
Unfavorable (your side only)	Lose 100	Lose 700

There is nothing special about going down two or four; other possible results could have been used to illustrate the same point. It isn't hard to see why so many of the unusual (or even outrageous) preempts described in Chapter 1 occurred when the vulnerability was favorable!

The exact level at which you should preempt depends on how conservative or aggressive you wish to be. This is dictated partly by the style that will make you most comfortable, which is a matter for you and your partner to decide, and partly by other factors that will be discussed in the following sections. Therefore the recommended guidelines allow you some leeway:

Vulnerability	*Overbid By:*		
	Conservative	*Standard Modern*	*Aggressive*
Favorable			
(opponents only)	3 tricks	4-5 tricks	6 or more tricks
Neither side	3 tricks	3-4 tricks	5 tricks
Both sides	2 tricks	3 tricks	3-4 tricks
Unfavorable			
(your side only)	2 tricks	2 tricks	2-3 tricks

The "conservative" course is simply the familiar Rule of Two and Three. The standard procedure among today's top players, however, is to increase the old-fashioned risk by at least one trick except at unfavorable vulnerability, where caution is still highly desirable. And some modern experts prefer to be even more aggressive than this.

Let's look at some examples:

(a)	♠	10 4	(b)	♠	7 5
	♡	K Q J 9 8 7 5		♡	Q
	◇	9		◇	10 5
	♣	9 6 3		♣	K Q 10 9 7 5 4 2

The player who held hand (a) in Deal 1 (Chapter 1) followed the conservative course; he opened with 3 ♡ at favorable vulnerability, and it worked. The standard modern approach, however, would be to open with 4 ♡ at this vulnerability. An aggressive player would also open with 4 ♡, since opening bids of five of a *major* are *not* used as preempts; the possibility of going down one when game could have been made by simply stopping at the four-level is too gruesome to risk.

With neither side vulnerable, the standard modern procedure is to open with either 4 ♡ or 3 ♡, depending on whether other factors (to be discussed in subsequent sections) point toward aggressiveness or conservatism. The aggressive approach is always to open with 4 ♡, while a conservative player would consistently opt for 3 ♡.

If both sides are vulnerable, standard modern calls for an opening bid of 3 ♡. An aggressive player would bid 4 ♡, while someone in search of conservatism would open with a *Weak Two-Bid* of 2 ♡. If you're not familiar with Weak Two-Bids, they work as follows: Opening bids of 2 ♢, 2 ♡, and 2 ♠ are just like three-level preempts, except that they promise one playing trick less (and are frequently based on only a six-card suit). When you have a rockcrusher, open with 2 ♣. This artificial and forcing bid tells partner not to pass; with nothing important to say, he bids 2 ♢ (artificial and "negative" or waiting). You now show your real suit, and the bidding proceeds normally. With the equivalent of a Weak Two-Bid in *clubs*, you must pass. Since strong two-bids rarely come up, it's silly to waste four bids on them, and they are now virtually obsolete among today's experts. (However, strong two-bids are still technically "standard," so don't throw a Weak Two-Bid at your partner unless you have agreed in advance to use this procedure.)

Finally, if the vulnerability is unfavorable, a Weak Two-Bid of 2 ♡ would be ample for all but the most aggressive preempter, who might insist on starting the proceedings with 3 ♡.

With hand (b), which arose in Deal 2, the standard modern practice is to open with 5 ♣ at favorable vulnerability; bid either 4 ♣ or 5 ♣ if neither side is vulnerable (the choice depends on the other factors that will be discussed shortly); open with 4 ♣ if both sides are vulnerable; and start off with 3 ♣ if the vulnerability is unfavorable. Aggressive players would open with 5 ♣ in all situations except unfavorable vulnerability, where 4 ♣ would be sufficient; conservative bidders would open with 4 ♣ when not vulnerable and bid 3 ♣ when vulnerable.

The following hands illustrate the standard modern procedure in action:

(a)   ♠   8 5   (b)   ♠   Q 10 8 6 5 3 2
       ♡   7 3   ♡   2
       ◇   10 9 2   ◇   J 10 8 5
       ♣   K Q 10 9 8 5   ♣   6

As we saw in deal 11, a 3 ♣ opening bid at favorable vulnerability is virtually automatic with hand (a). Similarly, 72 percent of an expert panel reported that they would bid 3 ♠ with hand (b), neither side vulnerable, even though the hand is worth only about five tricks and might take even less if disaster struck.

Preempting with hands like those in Deals 16-20, where the suits range from A 10 9 7 3 2 through Q J 7 6 4 3 (!) down to J 10 9 8 3 2 (!!) cannot be considered normal even by modern standards. If you choose to preempt with suits like these, you must consider yourself a highly aggressive bidder—and be prepared to pay accordingly when things go wrong.

YOUR POSITION AT THE TABLE

Preempts in *second* position should be somewhat more conservative than those made in first seat. Since one opponent has already passed, and since partner has not yet been heard from, your side may well own the balance of power. Thus an unusual preempt may only talk you out of your own makable game or slam.

Preempts in *third* position, however, can be quite uninhibited. Since partner has passed, your preempt won't catch him with a powerhouse and cause you to miss a laydown slam, so you may preempt with an unusual amount of defensive strength in the hope that the opponents will guess wrong:

(a)	(b)	(c)
♠ 6	♠ A 6	♠ A 6 3
♡ A K J 9 8 7 5	♡ K Q 10 8 7 6 2	♡ A Q J 10 7 6 2
◊ 5 4	◊ K 3	◊ Q 4
♣ A Q 7	♣ Q 5	♣ 6

All of these hands are mandatory 1 ♡ opening bids in first or second position, but a 4 ♡ preempt in third seat is not unreasonable.

Alternatively, if the first two players have passed and your hand is quite weak, it's a pretty good bet that the opponent on your left is happily adding up an impressive number of points—and eagerly hoping to have plenty of bidding room to describe his hand. In such cases, therefore, you may gain by being more aggressive, as happened in Deal 17:

♠ J 9 3
♡ 6 4
◊ Q 2
♣ A 10 9 7 3 2

Although the club suit is definitely substandard, the preempter did have two good things going for him: He was in third position and the vulnerability was favorable. He therefore opened with 3 ♣; and, since his madness was based on quite a bit of method, it is not too surprising that he registered a substantial gain. A similar good result was also achieved in Deal 8. When you are considering a preempt, therefore, be more aggressive if you are in third seat—especially if the opponents are vulnerable and you are not.

Preempts in *fourth* position are extremely rare. When made at the three-level, they tend to show a solid or nearly solid suit.

YOUR OPPONENTS' SKILL

It's always a good idea to size up your opponents as soon as possible, especially if you are playing a long match or session of rubber bridge against them. If they have demonstrated on the previous deal(s) that they have great difficulty coming within two tricks and three denominations of the right contract, it's silly to go out of your way to preempt. Why risk a penalty when they are going to get to the wrong spot all by themselves? Be conservative, and leave well enough alone unless you happen to have a classic "Rule of Two and Three" hand.

However, if your opponents are competent players, a more aggressive preemption policy is indicated. True, their defense will be better if they elect to double you, so it will be necessary to pick your spots well. But they are also much more likely to bid to the right contract if left to their own devices, and (as we have seen) even experts often have considerable difficulty overcoming a preempt.

YOUR OPPONENTS' BIDDING METHODS

Many players use doubles of preempts as cooperative ventures, allowing partner to bid or pass for penalties as his hand dictates. If your opponents use doubles primarily for penalties, you should be more conservative (and perhaps even adhere to the Rule of Two and Three). If their doubles of preempts are for takeout, requiring that partner bid his best suit, you can afford to be more aggressive. (We'll take a closer look at these methods for overcoming a preempt in Chapter 4.)

THE FORM OF SCORING

Be somewhat more conservative at rubber bridge than you would be in a "Swiss" or knockout team match. In a team game, every deal is a separate entity. Thus if you are set 700 points and the opponents could have made a 600-point game, your boldness will have cost you only 100 points. In rubber bridge, however, going down 700 when the opponents are vulnerable is worse, for the rubber will continue with you a game down and the opponents still poised to capture the 700-point rubber bonus. Therefore it's better to avoid paying out huge penalties for the privilege of continuing a rubber in which you are way behind.

At match points, small differences can have huge effects. If you go for 700 and everyone else in the room made 690 with the enemy cards, the innocuous-looking 10-point differential will cost you a cold bottom. Nevertheless, aggressive preempting is recommended at this form of scoring. Unlike rubber bridge, a disastrous penalty can be overcome on the next deal by making a mere overtrick more than everyone else, and you must try and induce the opponents to make mistakes against you if you are to have any chance to win. Be sure, however, to keep an eye on the vulnerability. If the opponents can only make a part score, going down two tricks vulnerable will be a disaster even if they fail to double.

If you happen to run into one of the few board-a-match team games still in existence, be conservative if your team is a good one; this is the worst form of scoring at which to fool around. Board-a-match is the most demanding of all events, so play down the middle and avoid throwing away boards that your teammates have all but won.

THE "STATE OF THE MATCH"

If you are playing in a team match and are clearly behind with not too many deals left to play, it is reasonable to try and generate a swing by preempting more aggressively. Don't carry this policy too far, however. Your teammates in the other room may be having a dream session, and they will have every right to be annoyed (and will probably never play with you again) if you have turned victory into defeat by making a zany preempt, down 1700, that never occurred to the player in the other room.

Even at match points, don't preempt wildly in the last few rounds unless you clearly have a chance to win the tournament by snagging a few last-minute tops. The players who are in contention will very much resent your altering the overall standings by gaily handing out top scores right and left, and any efficient tournament committee will also take a dim view of such shenanigans.

EXCEPTIONAL HOLDINGS

Two-suiters. The standard modern tendency is *not* to preempt with a two-suited hand. For example:

(a) ♠ —   (b) ♠ A K 10 8 6 2
     ♡ J 9 7 6 5   ♡ —
     ◇ 4   ◇ 10 7 6 5 4 2
     ♣ K Q 10 9 8 6 3   ♣ 3

An expert panel voted overwhelmingly to pass with hand (a) in second position, neither side vulnerable, and to pass with hand (b) in second position at unfavorable vulnerability.* To be sure, a preempt with a two-suiter could conceivably strike oil, as we saw in Deal 14; but unless conditions for preempting are extremely favorable, you will usually do better to seek an alternative call.

Side four-card majors. You are less likely to belong in your second suit if it is only four cards in length, so a preempt is more desirable in this situation. In fact, if your side four-card suit is a *minor*, a preemptive bid is perfectly acceptable. Today's experts, however, are divided as to whether or not to preempt with a side four-card *major* suit. For example, suppose you are in second seat at unfavorable vulnerability and hold:

                    ♠ —
                    ♡ A 6 5 3
                    ◇ K J 10 8 7 5 4 3
                    ♣ 8

What should you do? It's hard to make a mistake, for any reasonable action would find support from at least some experts. In an expert poll, the votes were:

                    12 for the pass
                    7 for 4 ◇
                    6 for 1 ◇
                    6 for 5 ◇
                    1 for 3 ◇

*There were some illustrious names in favor of a 4 ♣ preempt with hand (a), but almost no one opted to preempt with hand (b). In fact, the most popular bid among those experts who did elect to open with hand (b) was 1 ♠.

Thus over 40 percent of the panel opted to preempt in spite of the risk of missing a good heart contract; and in third position, or at favorable vulnerability, preempts might well have garnered a majority of the votes. Therefore, you are within your rights if you choose to preempt with a hand like this. An opening preempt is more dubious, however, with the hand shown in Deal 13:

```
♠  3
♡  Q 7 6 3
♢  A K Q J 8 5
♣  6 3
```

Even though the preempter was in third position, the actual 3 ♢ bid might well have missed a heart or notrump game that would have rolled home because of the solid diamond suit. A 1 ♢ opening bid would have provided more room for exploration and would hardly have lost much even on the actual deal, for North and South are cold for three of a red suit as the cards lie and can defeat an enemy 3 ♠ contract by at least one trick.

Minor suits headed by A K Q. There is little agreement among experts as to what to open with hands like these:

(a)	(b)	(c)
♠ 8 6	♠ 8 6	♠ 6 4
♡ J 5	♡ 3	♡ 4 3
♢ A K Q J 9 7 3	♢ A K Q J 7 4 3	♢ A K Q J 9 7 3 2
♣ 10 2	♣ J 8 2	♣ 3

An expert panel rejected a 3 ♢ preempt with hand (a), but a different panel voted slightly in favor of a 3 ♢ opening bid with hand (b). Thus the decision is one of tactics rather than rules. A preempt, a one-level opening bid, or even a pass could be the winning action; your decision must be based on the various factors discussed previously in this chapter. Hand (c) is from the Trials to select the 1971 U.S. International Team, and here's what actually happened:

West dealer
North-South vulnerable

```
                    NORTH
                    ♠  Q J 8 2
                    ♡  A K Q J
                    ◊  —
                    ♣  A Q 10 8 2
WEST                                      EAST
♠  6 4                                    ♠  K 10 9 7 5
♡  4 3                                    ♡  9 7 6
◊  A K Q J 9 7 3 2                        ◊  10 8 5
♣  3                                      ♣  7 5
                    SOUTH
                    ♠  A 3
                    ♡  10 8 5 2
                    ◊  6 4
                    ♣  K J 9 6 4
```

The bidding, Room 1:

SOUTH	WEST	NORTH	EAST
—	Pass	1 ♣	2 ♠
3 ♣	4 ◊	4 ♡	Pass
Pass	5 ◊	Pass	Pass
Double	Pass	5 ♡	Pass
Pass	Pass		

The bidding, Room 2:

SOUTH	WEST	NORTH	EAST
—	1 ◇	Double	1 ♠
2 ♡	3 ◇	4 ◇	5 ◇
6 ♣	6 ◇	6 ♡	Pass
Pass	7 ◇	Pass	Pass
7 ♡	Pass	Pass	Pass

In Room 1, West elected to pass in first position and achieved a good result when his opponents failed to reach their icy slam. The West player in Room 2 chose to open with 1 ◇; but, by the time he had rebid his suit at the six-level, his hand was an open book to everyone. The opponents therefore pushed on to slam; and although 7 ♡ needed quite a bit of luck, it turned out to be unbeatable. The opening spade lead was won by dummy's queen, East playing low, and declarer drew two rounds of trumps. He then played a club to his king, ruffed a diamond in dummy, returned to his hand with the ace of spades, and ruffed another diamond. He then led a low club to his jack; when West was unable to ruff, South drew the remaining trump and claimed his contract. After sadly scoring up this result, West (and his teammates in the other room) did indeed wish that he had opened with 5 ◇.

Major suits headed by A K Q. The modern tendency is to preempt with an absolutely solid *heart* suit, provided that there is no outside defensive strength. This has the advantage of making it harder for the opponents to get together (and outbid you) in the higher-ranking spade suit. With solid *spades*, more experts would favor a one-level opening because there is less danger of being outbid, but the majority would still opt to preempt. For example, a panel of experts voted to open with 4 ♠ in first position, both sides vulnerable, with:

♠ A K Q J 10 8 6 2
♡ 5 3
◇ 10
♣ J 6

Preemptive Overcalls

Preemptive overcalls are similar to preemptive opening bids. They show virtually the same kind of hand—a long, strong suit and little side defensive strength—and the same factors are important in determining when and how high to bid. Note, however, that it is highly desirable to have a respectable suit for your overcall. (See Deal 9.) Even if you are about to go down four, it will be hard for the opponents to elect to defend if one of them is looking at 6 4 2 in your suit and the other holds the singleton eight-spot. Your left-hand opponent, however, won't have to be a genius to double for penalties if his hand is bristling with honors in your suit, for he has heard his partner promise some defensive values by opening the bidding.

Suppose that neither side is vulnerable and you hold either of these hands:

(a)   ♠   K Q J 9 8 7 5   (b)   ♠   Q 7 6 5 4 3 2
      ♡   Q 3   ♡   A 10
      ♢   8 3 2   ♢   K 5
      ♣   8   ♣   7 6

If your right-hand opponent opens with 1 ♡, bid 3 ♠ with hand (a), just as you would when opening the bidding. An interesting if minor point is that your preempt may help score a trick for your queen of hearts if the opponents buy the hand and declarer has a two-way finesse, for he will probably play your partner for the missing side-suit high cards. With hand (b), however, a 1 ♠ overcall is sufficient. Your suit is shaky, and you have too much defensive strength for a preempt.

WEAK JUMP OVERCALLS

In standard bidding, a single jump overcall (such as a 2 ♠ overcall of a 1 ♡ opening bid) shows an extremely powerful hand. However, the majority of today's top players prefer to use Weak Jump Overcalls. WJOs show the same kind of hand as a Weak

Two-Bid, namely a preempt that is one trick shy of a three-level bid. The reason for using WJOs is similar to the rationale for abandoning strong opening two-bids: Rockcrushers calling for a strong jump overcall just don't occur very often, so it is better to adopt bidding weapons that you can use more frequently.

For example, suppose your right-hand opponent opens with 1 ♡ and you hold any of these hands:

(a) *Vul: Neither*	(b) *Vul: Both*	(c) *Vul: Opponents*
♠ A Q 10 9 7 6	♠ 5 2	♠ K 10 9 7 6 4
♡ 4 3	♡ Q 5	♡ 8 3
◇ 8 7 3	◇ J	◇ J 6
♣ J 8	♣ A Q 9 6 5 4 3 2	♣ Q 9 3

Hand (a) is a typical preempt, but only the most aggressive bidder would venture forth at the three-level. A Weak Jump Overcall of 2 ♠ is an ideal solution.

Some experts would overcall 4 ♣ with hand (b), but this is likely to result in a costly vulnerable penalty. A Weak Jump Overcall will bother the opponents almost as much and is noticeably safer, so the recommended call is 3 ♣.

With hand (c), the favorable vulnerability justifies aggressive actions, so you should bid 2 ♠. In addition to hindering the opponents, this will also tell partner that you are lacking defensive values and won't mind at all if he decides to sacrifice against an eventual enemy game or slam. When this hand took place in the 1967 U.S. Summer National Team of Four Championships, the Weak Jump Overcaller's partner was able to take a very profitable sacrifice in 6 ♠ (down only 1100). In the other room, the original overcall was only 1 ♠; neither player could then evaluate their side's defensive prospects, and they permitted the opponents to play in 7 ♡ and rack up 2210 points.

Weak Jump Overcalls can even be used over a strong notrump opening bid by the opponents, although a *very* strong suit is essential:

♠ A Q 10 9 8 7 4 3
♡ 4
◇ —
♣ 10 9 6 4

With neither side vulnerable, a 3 ♠ overcall is eminently correct and might well lead to a sizable gain—as we saw in Deal 10.

Rebids by the Preempter: A Cautionary Note

In most cases, *don't* bid again after making a preemptive bid. Your preempt has described your hand very accurately, so leave any future decisions to your partner; he knows roughly twice as much about your combined holdings as you do. The following is an excellent example of how *not* to preempt:

SOUTH	WEST	NORTH	EAST
3 ◇	3 ♡	4 ◇	4 ♡
5 ◇ ??	Double	Pass	Pass
Pass			

North actually had pretty good defensive values and was trying to lure the opponents into bidding just enough to go down, and he succeeded; they guessed wrong under the pressure, and 4 ♡ would have been defeated by at least one trick. South, however, decided to tell the same story twice, and cost his side a needless penalty. The moral: Tell your tale in one bid, and let partner take it from there. If you find that you are tempted to bid again later on, you probably should have preempted at a higher level at your first turn.

There are some rare instances, however, where it is correct for a preempter to take further action on his own. Since this falls under the heading of expert tactics, discussion will be deferred until Chapter 5.

Preemptive Ethics: The Skip-Bid Warning

The Skip-Bid Warning is a useful device for avoiding unpleasant arguments about hesitations and ethics in preemptive auctions. It is used in all important tournaments, and is strongly recommended for your home games as well.

To see why this procedure is desirable, suppose that you open with a preempt, your left-hand opponent thinks for a while and then passes, and your partner passes. Your right-hand opponent can now be quite sure that his partner has some important values (else why the hesitation?), which puts him in a touchy ethical position. The laws of bridge clearly state that a player must not make use of information obtained from the slowness or speed of his partner's actions, but even a highly honest player may have difficulty putting the hesitation entirely out of mind. Similarly, if your left-hand opponent passes your preempt like a shot, it will be hard for his partner to avoid being influenced by the obvious conclusion that a dubious entry into the auction will be most inadvisable.

The Skip-Bid Warning can help alleviate this painful situation. Here's how it works: A player making a preemptive bid announces, "I am about to make a skip bid. Please hesitate." He then makes his bid, and his left-hand opponent is obliged to pause for about ten seconds and pretend to be thinking even if he has a clear-cut pass. This makes it less likely that his partner will gain any inadvertent information, the strain on his partner's ethics will be reduced, and a happy ending for all concerned is very likely.

To be sure, the Skip-Bid Warning is no panacea. Some players, either out of ignorance or malevolence, ruin everything by passing instantly despite the warning, while certain wise guys stare at the ceiling and count off ten seconds in order to inform partner that they have no problem (and no high cards). A better procedure would be for the player to the left of the preemptive bidder to be barred from bidding until given permission (or "released") by the preempter; but this modification, which is used in Europe, is virtually unknown in this country.

Even if everyone is trying hard to be ethical, problems may still occur despite the Skip-Bid Warning. For example, suppose your left-hand opponent opens with 3 ♡ and, after thirty or forty seconds of agonized thought, your partner finally decides to pass. His hesitation is *not* censurable; bridge can be a pretty tough game, and no one can be expected to bid and play at the same speed in all instances —especially after a preempt. However, you can hardly fail to notice that he must have a pretty good hand. The solution is to refuse to take whatever action is indicated by his huddle unless it is clearly justified by your own holding; you should pass unless you obviously have enough strength to contest the issue on your own.*

Review Quiz

1. (a) What are the most favorable conditions for an opening preempt?
   (b) What are the least favorable conditions for an opening preempt?
   (c) What usually rules out an opening preempt?

2. In each of the following problems, you are using the "standard modern" procedure. What call would you make in first, second, and third positions? (Warning: Since preempting often involves questions of tactics and style, not all of the problems will have a single clear-cut right answer.)

(a)	*(b)*	*(c)*
Vul: Both	**Vul: None**	**Vul: None**
♠ 9 3 2	♠ 7	♠ A 6 2
♡ K Q J 9 6 5 3	♡ 5	♡ K Q 10 9 7 6 3
◊ J 6	◊ K J 10 8 7 6 3	◊ K J
♣ 8	♣ J 9 8 7	♣ 5

*Admittedly, it can be difficult to decide what represents a "clear-cut" action. *The Bridge World*, which has been a leading voice in the area of bridge ethics, has devoted considerable space to appropriate guidelines and examples. If in doubt, bend over backwards to take the action opposite to that indicated by the speed or slowness of partner's bid; you may get a poor score on occasion, but you'll win a lot of respect from knowledgeable bridge players.

(d)
Vul: Opponents
♠ 8 6
♡ 5
◇ A Q J 9 6 3
♣ J 8 5 4

(e)
Vul: You
♠ J 9 7 6 5 3 2
♡ 8 6
◇ K J 7
♣ 4

(f)
Vul: You
♠ 8 5
♡ A K Q J 9 7 6 3
◇ 7 5
♣ 3

(g)
Vul: Both
♠ K Q J 9 8 7
♡ 6 5 2
◇ K 5
♣ 10 7

(h)
Vul: Opponents
♠ A Q 10 9 8
♡ 6
◇ 8 7 4
♣ 10 9 7 6

(i)
Vul: You
♠ 7 3
♡ 6
◇ Q 9 7 4
♣ K Q 9 8 7 3

(j)
Vul: Opponents
♠ K 10 9 7
♡ 6
◇ 7 4
♣ A K Q J 6 5

(k)
Vul: Both
♠ Q J 10 9 7 6 4 2
♡ 7 2
◇ A 8
♣ J

(l)
Vul: Opponents
♠ 8 5
♡ 3
◇ J 8
♣ A Q J 10 7 6 5 2

3. Now suppose that your right-hand opponent has opened the bidding with 1 ♣. What call would you make with each of the preceding hands?

4. Use the following deal to explain why the Skip-Bid Warning is a highly desirable procedure:

South dealer
Both sides vulnerable

                        NORTH
                        ♠ J 5
                        ♡ K 3
                        ◇ K Q J 9
                        ♣ J 10 9 6 2
WEST   EAST
♠ A 9 8 7 6   ♠ K Q 4 2
♡ 6   ♡ 9 8 4
◇ A 10 4 3   ◇ 7 6 2
♣ K 7 5   ♣ A Q 8
                        SOUTH
                        ♠ 10 3
                        ♡ A Q J 10 7 5 2
                        ◇ 8 5
                        ♣ 4 3

5. What call do you make in the following problem? Neither
side is vulnerable.

YOU   LHO   PARTNER   RHO   You hold:
3 ♠   4 ♡   4 ♠   5 ♡   ♠ K J 10 9 8 6 4 3
   ?   ♡ 7 3
                                         ◇ 4 2
                                         ♣ 6

Solutions

1. (a) The opponents are vulnerable and you are not, you are in third position, and the opponents use doubles of preempts strictly for takeout. The need to create a swing when behind is also a factor to consider, although this is often overdone by players who fail to realize that the most likely result of a foolish preempt is a serious backfire.

(b) You are vulnerable and the opponents are not, you are in second position, and the opponents use doubles of preempts strictly for penalties. In addition, shaky preempts are somewhat less desirable against opponents who are poor constructive bidders (and hence likely to get to the wrong spot even if left alone), at rubber bridge (where vulnerable opponents will retain their advantage on the next deal), and when you are comfortably ahead and expect to win barring some hideous debacle.

(c) A lot of outside defensive strength or a very weak suit.

2. (a) *Three hearts (all positions).* You have a fine suit and poor defensive values, and are within the accepted modern standard of three tricks of your bid with both sides vulnerable.

(b) *Three diamonds (all positions).* This is a clear-cut modern opening three-bid with neither side vulnerable, even though the hand might take only five tricks if things go badly. In fact, the 3 ♢ opening bid is not unreasonable even if both sides are vulnerable.

(c) *One heart in first or second position, one heart or four hearts in third position.* You have far too much defensive strength for a preempt in first or second position, so the 1 ♡ bid is the only acceptable choice. In third seat, however, you are very unlikely to have a slam in view of partner's original pass, so you may (if you wish) try to confound the opponents with a tactical 4 ♡ preempt. They may well guess wrong under the pressure and do something disastrous, especially in view of your unexpected defensive strength. The risk is that you will get too high when the hand actually belongs to you in a part-score contract, or when no one can make much of anything.

(d) *Two or three diamonds in first position, two diamonds in second position, and three diamonds in third position.* In second position, where one opponent has announced weakness by passing and partner has yet to be heard from, the Weak Two-Bid is your best choice. Greater aggressiveness is desirable in third seat, however, because partner has also passed. And in first position, the choice depends on the other factors discussed in this chapter.*

(e) *Pass (all positions).* Preempting with a weak suit at unfavorable vulnerability might work out well on any one deal, but in the long run will ensure your placing high on everyone's Most Popular Opponents list.

(f) *Four hearts (all positions).* You need this much strength to preempt at the four-level when the vulnerability is unfavorable. Some experts might open with 1 ♡ and some might lie in wait by making a tactical pass, but the preempt is preferable in view of your lack of defensive strength.

(g) *Two spades (all positions).* A typical Weak Two-Bid—a strong six-card suit and not too much defensive strength.

(h) *Pass in first or second position, pass or two spades in third position.* Normally, a Weak Two-Bid requires at least a six-card suit in order to provide the necessary margin of safety. Heroic measures are not unreasonable, however, when you are in third position at favorable vulnerability.

(i) *Pass (all positions).* At unfavorable vulnerability, leave the heroic measures to the suicide squad. If the vulnerability were favorable, a 3 ♣ preempt would be acceptable (although aggressive), especially if you are in third position.

(j) *One club (all positions).* The risk of missing a good notrump or spade contract by preempting is too great.

(k) *Four spades (all positions).* With seven sure tricks, a 3 ♠ preempt would be rather conservative by modern standards.

---

*When in doubt, follow the more conservative course of action, since "standard modern" is somewhat on the aggressive side.

(l) *Five clubs (all positions).* Since the vulnerability is favorable, try to create as much trouble as possible for the opponents. If both sides were vulnerable, a 4 ♣ preempt would be preferable.

3. Since preemptive overcalls are similar in many respects to preemptive opening bids, many of the previous answers remain correct.

(a) *Three hearts.* Conservatism is often more desirable when making a preemptive *overcall*, for the opening bid will make it easier for your left-hand opponent to double for penalties. When you have such a fine suit, however, you should get the full mileage out of your preempt.

(b) *Three diamonds.* Since you are not vulnerable, you don't need quite as strong a suit to overcall at the three-level.

(c) *One heart.* A tactical 4 ♡ overcall is conceivable if partner has passed originally, but it has less to gain (and is more dangerous) since the opponents have already gotten a word in.

(d) *Two or three diamonds.* It is reasonable to be somewhat more conservative than when opening the bidding since your suit is only six cards in length, but a 3 ◇ overcall at this vulnerability is quite acceptable.

(e) *Pass.* Your suit is too weak.

(f) *Four hearts.* Despite the vulnerability, anything less would be distinctly timid in view of your eight solid tricks.

(g) *One or two spades.* The Weak Jump Overcall has the advantage of telling partner that your defensive strength is limited, while the 1 ♠ overcall is safer and describes your hand reasonably well.

(h) *One or two spades.* The normal action is a 1 ♠ over-call. It will achieve at least some preemption since your left-hand opponent can no longer respond 1 ◇ or 1 ♡, and non-vulnerable overcalls don't guarantee a great deal of high cards. However, if you favor aggressiveness at favorable vulnerability, insert a club with your spades and make a Weak Jump Overcall of 2 ♠ (especially if partner has passed originally). This will inform partner that your defensive prospects are pretty grim, and will do more to disrupt the enemy bidding machinery.

(i) *Pass*. A 3 ♣ overcall actually would be a Weak Jump Overcall since many players open with short minor suits, but the vulnerability prohibits any action.

(j) *Pass*. There is no good bid available.

(k) *Four spades*. A more conservative 3 ♠ overcall has merit but might well allow the opponents to find a good heart fit.

(l) *Five clubs*. As in Question 2, a 4 ♣ preempt would be sufficient if both sides were vulnerable.

4. South will open with a preempt in hearts (probably 3 ♡, possibly 4 ♡), and this will give West something to think about. Eventually, he may well decide not to risk entering the auction at a high level. If he does hesitate noticeably and pass, East will have *quite* an ethical problem. If he bids, he is perhaps being influenced by information that he is ethically obliged to ignore (his partner's huddle, which must indicate some respectable values). And if he passes, he is likely to feel as though he is penalizing himself for being honest.

If South properly announces a "skip bid," however, West must wait at least ten seconds (and pretend to be thinking) before acting, even if he has a Yarborough. If he reaches a decision shortly thereafter, East will have no way of obtaining any improper information and will be free to be conservative or aggressive as he sees fit.

If West hesitates for thirty or forty seconds and then passes, however, even the Skip-Bid Warning will not keep East from noticing that his partner must have a pretty good hand. Therefore East should *pass*. His hand is borderline at best, so he is obliged to bend over backwards to do the opposite of what is suggested by his partner's huddle.

5. *Pass*. Perhaps you should have opened with 4 ♠ originally, but it's too late to change your mind now. Partner knows your approximate holding and is therefore in charge of the auction, and he may be trying to set a trap for the opponents with some reasonable defensive values. Don't get in his way by telling the same story twice!

3

Responding to Partner's Preempt

♠ ♡ ◇ ♣

A preempt, as we have seen, is a highly descriptive bid. When your partner preempts, therefore, *you are in charge of the auction*, and it is up to you to guide your side to the proper contract.

Since partner's preempt announces a primarily one-suited hand, you should usually (though not always) forget about playing in any of your own suits and concentrate on the one he has advertised. Also, do not hasten to pass simply because your hand is fairly weak. Partner has indicated he doesn't see much hope of defeating an enemy contract; if your own defensive strength is limited, it may be an excellent idea to increase the pressure on your opponents by raising the level of bidding. In fact, even a single raise may deprive them of crucial bidding room and nudge them into a horrendous contract.

Responding to an Opening Preempt

RAISES BASED ON STRENGTH

If partner's preempt catches you with a powerful hand, you don't need to worry about blockading the opponents. Instead, your main task will be to determine how much your side can make. This requires that you keep the vulnerability in mind and count *tricks* instead of points. For example, suppose that neither side is vulnerable, partner deals and opens with 3 ♡, and you hold any of these hands:

63

(a)	(b)	(c)
♠ A K J 2	♠ K Q 9	♠ K 10 4
♡ 7	♡ 7	♡ 7
◇ A K 9 4	◇ A J 9 8	◇ A Q 9 8 7 6 2
♣ J 10 3 2	♣ Q J 10 6 2	♣ Q 8

Partner's three-level preempt in first position, with neither side vulnerable, promises about five or six tricks. Hand (a) will provide four or five more, so the probable total is ten and you should raise to 4 ♡. If you respond 3 NT simply because you have all the unbid suits stopped, you are likely to wind up in serious trouble. Remember that partner's typical hand is:

> ♠ 7 6 5
> ♡ K Q J 9 8 6 3
> ◇ 10
> ♣ 7 5

If you play in notrump, you'll be cut off from his long suit and suffer a desperate shortage of tricks. Even a doubleton heart in your hand would not be sufficient to justify a bid of 3 NT, for your wily opponents will surely hold up the ace of hearts for one round if necessary to permanently strand the long hearts in dummy.

With hand (b) you should pass. Your two or three tricks don't figure to be enough for game opposite the five or six tricks partner has promised, especially since your poor heart fit precludes a notrump contract. Since partner's preempt denies much in the way of side-suit strength, and since you have only one ace and one king, the opponents can probably take a lot of tricks in a hurry. For example, if partner has the hand shown above, even 3 ♡ is in jeopardy. A good rule to keep in mind is that side-suit queens and jacks usually don't help much opposite a preempt.

Also pass with hand (c), for game is undoubtedly out of reach. Partner's suit should be as good as yours, and his diamond support might be even worse. He's on your side, and fighting with him can only enrich the opponents.

A vulnerable preempt promises somewhat more strength, so you need somewhat less to raise to game. For example, suppose that partner opens with 3 ♠ in first position, both sides are vulnerable, and you hold either of these hands:

(a)   ♠   Q 2   (b)   ♠   4
           ♡   A 8 5 2   ♡   K Q 8 4
           ◇   10 7 4   ◇   K Q 3 2
           ♣   A K 7 3   ♣   Q J 6 2

This preempt shows about six or seven tricks and hand (a) is worth about three and a half tricks, so game is clearly on the horizon. A bid of 3½ ♠, however, will surely run afoul of the authorities (and your opponents), so you should raise to 4 ♠. You'll be in fine shape if partner has:

     ♠   A K 10 9 7 6 5
     ♡   7
     ◇   9 8 6
     ♣   8 5

Even if the king of spades is changed to the jack, giving partner a light but reasonable preempt, you still have the spade finesse for your contract. To be sure, you *will* be in a hopeless contract if partner elected to preempt with seven spades to the king-jack, but this is one of the risks inherent in preemptive bidding: When your side actually owns the hand, you may have to guess what to do (and may well guess wrong) at a high level of bidding.

With hand (b), however, you should pass. You have too few quick tricks to risk 4 ♠, and your singleton spade rules out a no-trump contract. If partner has the example hand shown above, even 3 ♠ could easily go down.

If partner opens with a game-level preempt and the trick count indicates that slam is out of reach, simply pass and hope to chalk up your contract. For example (both sides vulnerable):

(a)   Partner opens 4 ♡   (b)   Partner opens 5 ◊
       ♠ A 8 6 3   ♠ K 7 6 4
       ♡ 7 2   ♡ A 5 4
       ◊ A 9 7 5   ◊ 8
       ♣ A 6 2   ♣ A 7 6 3 2

Don't be overawed by your high cards! The most you can reasonably expect opposite hand (a) is eight solid hearts, which will leave you a trick short of slam; and you will be *very* happy to remain in 4 ♡ if partner happens to have a seven-trick hand like:

                    ♠ 7 4
                    ♡ K Q J 10 8 6 5 3
                    ◊ 4
                    ♣ J 7

Similarly, partner is unlikely to have more than nine solid diamonds opposite hand (b), which would make slam a 50-50 proposition at best, and he could easily have less. Therefore your best choice in both cases is to pass.

If the trick count indicates that you are in the slam range, matters become more complex. Slam bidding after a preempt can be a tricky proposition, so it will be discussed in a section of its own later in this chapter.

When responding to partner's preempt, be sure to keep in mind the various factors that affect the strength of his hand. In addition, a knowledge of his preemptive habits will also be helpful. Thus if you know that he is addicted to light preempts at favorable vulnerability, give him some leeway if you have a borderline hand. If you know that he always adheres to the Rule of Two and Three, you can raise with somewhat less than is needed opposite a player using the "standard modern" approach. Don't carry this too far, however. If you have a clear-cut action, take it—and let partner take the responsibility for your result if he has made an unusual preempt.

TACTICAL RAISES AND ADVANCE SACRIFICES

If you have a modicum of support for partner's suit and your defensive values are limited, it may be a good idea to aid his preemptive tactics by pushing the auction up a notch or two. Good support, while desirable, is not essential since he has promised an excellent suit; and the opponents undoubtedly have a good thing somewhere—*if* they can find it. For example, suppose that partner deals and opens with 3 ♠, the next player passes, and you hold:

> ♠ 8 6 3
> ♡ 5
> ♦ K 10 7 6
> ♣ A J 5 4 2

Regardless of the vulnerability, you should raise to 4 ♠. Partner is unlikely to have more than one defensive trick. Thus the opponents should be cold for 4 ♡, and your ace of clubs and ruffing value in hearts should be worth several tricks in support. If the defensive strength is evenly divided, each opponent may think that you are raising because you have a powerful hand and expect to make 4 ♠. If they are afraid to enter the auction, you will get away with a trivial penalty when they have an easy game. And even if the opponents decide to double, nothing will have been lost, for you will surely have a profitable sacrifice in 4 ♠ doubled. The *advance sacrifice* (taken *before* the opponents find their best contract) enables you to have your cake and consume it also; it gets you to the right spot at once, and creates so much confusion in the enemy camp that they may well commit a disastrous blunder.

Here are some more examples, this time from Chapter 1:

(a)	(b)	(c)
Deal 15	Deal 17	Deal 20
♠ J 7 3	♠ K 7 2	♠ J 9 8
♡ A K 5 2	♡ Q 9	♡ K 8
♦ 9 5 3 2	♦ K 9 8 5	♦ J 10 8 3 2
♣ 6 4	♣ Q 8 6 4	♣ 5 4 2

The player who held hand (a) heard his partner open with 3 ♠ in first seat, neither side vulnerable, and the next player overcalled with 4 ♣. He sized up his two sure tricks and good spade support and promptly bid 4 ♠, which succeeded in pushing the enemy one trick too high.

After partner opened Deal 17 with 3 ♣ in third position (favorable vulnerability) and the next player passed, the player with hand (b) wisely increased the pressure by raising to 4 ♣. The opponents could not cope with this additional obstruction, and wound up in a hopeless contract.

In hand (c), partner dealt and opened with 3 ♣ at favorable vulnerability, and the next player overcalled with 3 ◇. The player with these cards decided that his club support, side king, and ruffing values in hearts made a 4 ♣ bid reasonably safe at this vulnerability, and the raise helped bring about a very successful outcome.

(d)	(e)	(f)
Deal 11	Deal 19	Deal 25
♠ 4 3	♠ 7 5 4	♠ K 9 2
♡ J 10 9 2	♡ A 6	♡ K 8
◇ J 7 6 3	◇ J 10 4 2	◇ 10 9 8 5
♣ A 4 2	♣ A Q 9 5	♣ J 10 9 7

Deal 11 occurred in a team game, and both players with hand (d) heard partner open with 3 ♣ at favorable vulnerability. After an intervention by right-hand opponent (3 ♠ in one room, 4 ♣ in the other), they both chose to bid 5 ♣ with the hope of confounding their vulnerable opponents. And they both succeeded, for a hopeless slam was reached in each case.

The player with hand (e) also helped jockey his opponents into a losing slam contract. His partner dealt and opened with 3 ♠ at favorable vulnerability, and his right-hand opponent doubled. He inserted a bid of 4 ♠, and was highly gratified when the opponents then blundered into 6 ♡ and his two aces cashed.

The player who held hand (f) heard his partner open with 3 ♣ in first position, at favorable vulnerability. The next player passed, and he jumped to 5 ♣. As a result, his opponents reached a terrible slam—but in this case they made it, proving that virtue (and skillful preemptive bidding) does not always triumph!

Raising can be such a thorn in the enemy's side that some

players get into the act even with inferior values or poor support for partner's suit. Sometimes this works out well:

(Deal 8)
♠ 9 5 2
♡ K J 10 5 2
♢ 10 5 3
♣ Q 10

After partner opened with 3 ♣ in third position (favorable vulnerability) and the next player overcalled with 3 ♢, the player with these cards raised to 4 ♣! It worked, for the opponents reached a hideous 4-2 heart fit when they could easily have made game elsewhere. However, such raises may also work out rather poorly:

(Deal 4)
♠ J 10 6
♡ A J 5
♢ A J 10 4 2
♣ 10 3

Partner dealt and opened with 3 ♣ at favorable vulnerability, and the next player doubled. At this point the opponents were in serious trouble; anything they bid would have gone down quite a few, and 3 ♣ doubled would have made easily. But the player with these cards got them off the hook by raising to 4 ♣. (Perhaps the fact that they got back on again by doubling 4 ♣, but not defeating it, partially vindicates his decision.)

Raising with poor trump support, then, is a debatable issue. However, it is clear that when you do decide to raise, you should *make your maximum preempt at once* and then subside, just as you would when opening the bidding. For example:

♠ K J 9 6
♡ 10 9 3
♢ A 5 4 3 2
♣ 7

The vulnerability is favorable, partner opens with 3 ♠, and the next player chimes in with 4 ♡. The opponents are not yet in slam, but can there be much doubt that they will get there—and make it? Your spade length should rule out any tricks in that suit even if partner has the ace. Thus your only defensive winner rates to be the ace of diamonds. If you bid 4 ♠ now and sacrifice in 6 ♠ later, you'll be giving the opponents a chance to exchange information at the five-level, so jump to 6 ♠ right away! This will cost you an extra 200 points if partner turns up with a defensive trick, since a 5 ♠ sacrifice would have been adequate. But it is worth the risk, for you may well push the enemy into a hopeless grand slam by leaving them only one round of bidding in which to operate.

Here's an example of an advance sacrifice that occurred in a 1968 match between the United States and Canada, with both sides showing excellent judgment:

South dealer
East-West vulnerable

```
                        NORTH
                        ♠  10 7
                        ♡  J 9 5
                        ◇  A 6 5 3
                        ♣  A J 9 2
        WEST                                EAST
        ♠  A K 9 8 3                         ♠  Q J 6 2
        ♡  K Q 8 3                           ♡  A 10 7 6 2
        ◇  Q 8 2                             ◇  J 7
        ♣  7                                 ♣  Q 8
                        SOUTH
                        ♠  5 4
                        ♡  4
                        ◇  K 10 9 4
                        ♣  K 10 6 5 4 3
```

The bidding:

SOUTH	WEST	NORTH	EAST
3 ♣	Double	5 ♣	Double
Pass	Pass	Pass	

North put maximum pressure on the opponents by jumping directly to 5 ♣, thereby reaching an excellent sacrifice against their vulnerable game. East gauged the situation well by refusing to go on to (and go down in) 5 ♡ or 5 ♠; he doubled and took what points he could still get (300 for down two, rather than 620 for making a major-suit game).

The following deal provides a particularly good illustration of how to (and how not to) respond to a preempt:

East dealer
North-South vulnerable

```
                    NORTH
                    ♠  A Q 8 6 4 2
                    ♡  5 4
                    ◇  10 7 3 2
                    ♣  A
WEST                                        EAST
♠  9 7                                      ♠  J 3
♡  A K 9 8 3                                ♡  J 10 2
◇  J 5                                      ◇  4
♣  J 10 7 2                                 ♣  K Q 9 8 5 4 3
                    SOUTH
                    ♠  K 10 5
                    ♡  Q 7 6
                    ◇  A K Q 9 8 6
                    ♣  6
```

The bidding, Room 1:

SOUTH	WEST	NORTH	EAST
—	—	—	3 ♣
3 ◇	3 ♡	3 ♠	Pass
4 ♠	5 ♣	5 ♠	Pass
Pass	6 ♣	Pass	Pass
Double	Pass	Pass	Pass

The bidding, Room 2:

SOUTH	WEST	NORTH	EAST
—	—	—	3 ♣
3 ◇	6 ♣	6 ◇	Pass
Pass	Pass		

In Room 1, West selfishly decided to bid his own suit. This let North show his spades cheaply, and the resulting exchange of information helped North-South guess correctly (and collect 500 points) when West ultimately sacrificed in clubs.

In Room 2, however, West properly took an immediate advance sacrifice by bidding 6 ♣. North, under pressure, can hardly be blamed for bidding 6 ◇, and West quickly cashed his high hearts to register a plus score for his side.

To sum up: When partner's preempt and your own meager values indicate that the opponents can make quite a lot if left to their own devices, and when the vulnerability permits, insert a raise or even take an advance sacrifice if you have some support for partner's suit and a high card or two on the side. Usually your best strategy will be to make your maximum preempt at once, thereby depriving the opponents of as much bidding room as possible and making them guess at a very high level of bidding. Be reasonably sure, however, that a doubled penalty will prove to be a good investment, for good opponents are likely to take a sure plus score rather than fumble around for the best contract at the six-level.

NOTRUMP RESPONSES

There are two main kinds of hands that call for a 3 NT response to a three-level preempt by your partner. To illustrate, suppose that neither side is vulnerable, partner starts off with 3 ♠, and you hold either of these hands:

(a)   ♠   8
      ♡   K Q J
      ◇   K Q 10
      ♣   A K Q J 8 3

(b)   ♠   J 10 8
      ♡   A K 10
      ◇   Q J 10 9
      ♣   K Q J

With hand (a) your best chance for game is in notrump. A 4 ♠ contract could easily be wrecked by a poor trump split, and 5 ♣ might well be defeated because the opponents can cash three aces. Partner's hand:

     ♠   K Q 9 7 6 4 2
     ♡   7 3
     ◇   6 4
     ♣   4 2

Hand (b) is quite powerful but suffers from a shortage of aces and kings, so the opponents might well be able to take the first four tricks in a 4 ♠ contract. Your balanced distribution and numerous stoppers in the side suits are ideal for notrump play, and your spade fit makes it very unlikely that the opponents can cut you off from dummy. Therefore your best response is 3 NT. Note that unless you intend to make 3 NT on your own steam, as in hand (a), you should not play in notrump unless you have a good fit for partner's suit.

Notrump bidding can often be quite a problem for players who favor indiscriminate preempts. Opener is expected to pass your 3 NT response regardless of his hand; he has already shown his long

suit and meager strength, so he must trust your judgment (and your
choice of the final contract). This can be difficult, however, when
he has blithely opened on seven to the jack and suspects that you
will be highly disappointed with the quality of his suit.

The other end of the scale can also cause severe difficulties.
Suppose partner deals and opens with 3 ◇, both sides vulnerable,
and you hold:

♠   Q J 8 2
♡   A 6 4
◇   7 2
♣   A 7 6 2

You should pass. A notrump game will be hopeless opposite a
typical preempt like:

♠   7
♡   5 3
◇   K Q 10 9 6 5 4
♣   8 4 3

The opponents will simply set up one of their suits, hold up the
ace of diamonds for one round, and send 3 NT down a gory five or
six tricks. However, it will be highly disconcerting to play in 3 ◇
and find partner with:

♠   7
♡   5 3
◇   A K Q J 9 8 6
♣   8 4 3

This is why many players refuse to preempt with an absolutely solid minor. They prefer to reach their laydown notrump game with an auction such as:

Opener	Responder
1 ◇	1 ♠
2 ◇	2 NT
3 NT	Pass

Because of problems like these, some players have even gone so far as to develop specialized asking bids over partner's 3 ♣ and 3 ◇ preempts in order to find out just how strong his suit actually is. A simpler plan, and an effective one in most situations, is to open with *one* of your minor when it is headed by A K Q and to *pass* with a poor suit unless conditions for preempting are extremely favorable.

In some situations, certain Mad Scientists use a psychic 3 NT response in an attempt to bewilder the opponents; this tactic is discussed in Chapter 5. Responses of 4 NT and 5 NT are conventional and fall under the rubric of slam bidding, to be discussed later in this chapter.

NEW-SUIT RESPONSES

New-suit responses to a preemptive opening bid are relatively infrequent. A new suit at the *three*-level is forcing and urges partner to raise your suit with the slightest excuse. (Three small cards or a doubleton honor is sufficient.) If partner cannot raise, he should show a side-suit stopper if he can do so at the three-level, since 3 NT might be the best contract. Otherwise, he returns to four of his suit. For example, if partner deals and opens with 3 ♣, neither side vulnerable, respond 3 ♡ holding:

♠ A 3 2
♥ A Q J 6 4 2
♦ A K 8
♣ 7

A response of four of a *minor* to an opening bid of 3 ♥ or
3 ♠, or a 4 ♣ response to a 3 ♦ opening bid, is forcing and is
usually a slam try. It presumably agrees on opener's suit as the
trump suit, and invites him to show any useful features that he may
have (such as a side-suit ace or king, or support for responder's
suit). Sometimes, however, this response may be lead-directional in
nature:

♠ K Q 8 6 4
♥ 7 4 3 2
♦ —
♣ 7 6 5 4

If partner deals and opens with 3 ♠ at favorable vulnerability
and the next player doubles, some theorists would bid 4 ♦ in case
partner is on opening lead against an eventual club or heart contract
by the enemy. There is no danger of being left to play in 4 ♦
undoubled at this vulnerability, but there is a serious risk of tipping
off the opponents in time for them to make certain that you are on
opening lead (or to play in diamonds). Against good players, therefore, better results may be achieved by jumping directly to 6 ♠. If
your left-hand opponent now bids 7 ♥, you can double to advise
partner of the need for an unusual opening lead.

A response of 4 ♥ or 4 ♠, as a new-suit bid, expresses a
desire to play in that contract. It shows a very strong suit and
suggests that the major-suit game will be preferable to game in
opener's minor suit.

New-suit bids at the *five*-level are a hazy subject even among
experts. Since these bids are quite rare, special meanings will be
recommended in the section on slam bidding that follows.

SLAM BIDDING

In this section we will consider some procedures for getting to the right spot when partner opens with a preempt and you have a real powerhouse. None of the following conventions are hard to learn, but if you elect to use any, be sure to discuss them thoroughly in advance with your partner. Even experts have had costly bidding misunderstandings because they got their signals mixed, and slam bidding after a preempt is unfamiliar ground for most players.

The Blackwood Convention. A response of 4 NT to an opening bid of three or four of a suit is the familiar Blackwood ace-asking convention. Since a preempt usually denies much in the way of aces, and since Blackwood is desirable only when you will know exactly what to do after hearing partner's answer, opportunities for the direct use of Blackwood over partner's preempt are relatively infrequent. The following hand would qualify:

$$\begin{aligned}
&\spadesuit \quad K \ 8 \ 6 \ 3 \\
&\heartsuit \quad A \ K \ Q \ J \ 4 \ 3 \\
&\diamondsuit \quad 8 \\
&\clubsuit \quad A \ K
\end{aligned}$$

If partner opens with 3 ♠ or 4 ♠, your fine spade support should rule out any possibility of a secondary trump loser. Therefore the only crucial issue is the number of aces residing in partner's hand, and you should respond 4 NT. If partner shows no aces, sign off in 5 ♠; if he has one ace, bid 6 ♠; if he turns up with two aces, proceed directly to 7 NT.

The Direct Grand Slam Force. The lesser known but extremely useful Grand Slam Force asks about *the top three honors in partner's suit*, and is an excellent way to ensure that you have all the high trumps before risking a seven-level contract. To put it into operation, bid 5 NT directly over partner's opening preempt. He answers as follows:

6 ♣ = none of the top three honors (his suit
     is jack-high or worse)*

6 of his suit = one of the top three honors (his suit
     is headed by A *or* K *or* Q)

7 ♣ = two of the top three honors (his suit is
     headed by AK *or* AQ *or* KQ)

Some players bid seven of the long suit with two of the top three honors, but 7 ♣ is preferable just in case the Grand Slam Force bidder actually wants to play the hand somewhere else. (For example, he may have an absolutely solid suit of his own.) An alternative system of responses that does have considerable merit is to use 6 NT to show two of the top three honors and 7 ♣ to show all three of them. As with Blackwood, the 5 NT bidder is in complete charge of the auction, and partner must pass his next bid.

Here's an example:

♠ Q 8 4
♡ A K Q J 4 3
◇ —
♣ A K 7 2

Both sides are vulnerable, and partner opens with 3 ♠ or 4 ♠. It should be safe to assume that his suit is better than seven to the jack, so respond 5 NT. If he bids 6 ♠, indicating that the ace or king of spades is missing, you will pass and be in a fine slam. (At worst, it will depend on a 2-1 trump split.) And if he bids 7 ♣, showing that he has the ace and king of spades, you can confidently bid 7 ♠. Note that Blackwood would be a very poor choice in this situation; if partner turned up with one ace and one king, you would

*Players who prefer not to preempt with jack-high suits or worse, and hence will always have at least the queen, can use the following responses: 6 ♣ shows the queen (only), 6 of opener's long suit shows the ace or king, and 7 ♣ shows two of the top three honors. This, of course, requires a firm partnership agreement in advance.

have no way to determine whether they were in spades or in diamonds.

The Delayed Grand Slam Force. Suppose that both sides are vulnerable, partner deals and opens with 4 ♠, and you hold:

♠ A
♡ A K Q 8 4 3
♢ 2
♣ A K 7 5 2

You decide to check for aces by bidding 4 NT, and partner responds 5 ♢. What now?

Grand slam will be a good bet if partner has the king and queen of spades. However, a 5 NT bid at this point would be a Blackwood inquiry about the number of kings in his hand, and that wouldn't tell you much about his all-important spade holding. Therefore many players use a 6 ♣ bid by the Blackwood 4 NT bidder as the Grand Slam Force. Partner answers as follows:

6 ♢ = none of the top three honors
6 of his suit = one of the top three honors
7 ♣ = two of the top three honors

(If his suit is diamonds, a 6 ♢ response is ambiguous and shows either none or one of the top three honors.) If partner responds 6 ♠ to your 6 ♣ Grand Slam Force, you will know that the opponents have a high spade and that you should therefore pass. But if partner has both the king and the queen of spades, he will bid 7 ♣ and you will return to 7 ♠ (*not* 7 NT, as an enemy diamond lead could cut you off from partner's hand while your singleton ace of spades still blocks the suit).

Keep in mind that the Delayed Grand Slam Force of 6 ♣ is used only when, for whatever reason, a Direct Grand Slam Force of 5 NT was not possible, and when partner's long suit is either a major or diamonds (not clubs!).

The Control Asking Bid. Suppose partner deals and opens with
4 ♠, neither side vulnerable, and you hold:

$$\begin{array}{ll} ♠ & A\ Q\ 4 \\ ♡ & A\ K \\ ◊ & A\ K\ Q\ 9\ 7 \\ ♣ & Q\ J\ 3 \end{array}$$

You could jump to slam and hope that the opponents fail to
lead clubs, but they are unlikely to be so obliging. Yet if you pass,
partner may turn up with a singleton or even a void in clubs. Alternatively, you can try Blackwood—and then consult your horoscope
or lucky star in the likely event that partner doesn't have any aces.

Fortunately, a better plan is available. Since hands calling for a
new-suit response at the five-level are about as frequent as eclipses
during snowstorms in July, you can use five-level responses as
Control Asking Bids. For example, bid 5 ♣ with the above hand,
asking partner whether or not he can prevent a catastrophe in the
club suit. He answers as follows:

First step above your asking bid = no controls in the
  asked suit (opponents can take the first two tricks)
Second step above your asking bid = second-round control
  (king or singleton) in the asked suit
Third step above your asking bid = first-round control
  (ace or void) in the asked suit

Matters are now quite simple. If your 5 ♣ bid produces an
answer of 5 ◊, you will know that there are two club losers and that
you should sign off in 5 ♠. If partner bids 5 ♡ instead, showing a
singleton club or the king (but not the ace), you can safely contract
for 6 ♠. And if he bids 5 ♠, showing the ace or a void in clubs,
you can go straight to 7 ♠.

Situations like this have come up several times in World
Championship play, and have frequently cost U.S. teams a bundle
of points. Here's an example from the 1972 World Championships:

Opener	*Responder*
♠ K Q J 10 9 8 2	♠ A 6 4
♡ Q J 9 4	♡ A K
◇ —	◇ K J 3
♣ 5 4	♣ A K 7 6 2

When the U.S. held these cards, opener bid 4 ♠. Responder tried Blackwood and stopped in 6 ♠ when opener denied any aces. Control Asking Bids would have done better:

Opener	*Responder*
4 ♠	5 ◇ (a)
5 NT (b)	6 ♣ (c)
7 ♣ (d)	7 ♠ (e)
Pass	

(a) Control Asking Bid.
(b) Three steps above the asking bid, and hence first-round control in diamonds.
(c) Since 5 NT is no longer available, responder trots out the Delayed Grand Slam Force. (As always, it's a good idea to discuss this with partner in advance, or else you may wind up playing 6 ♣!)
(d) Two of the top three spade honors.
(e) Not 7 NT, since opener's first-round diamond control may be a void.

In the 1973 World Championships, the U.S. team did even worse:

Opener	*Responder*
♠ K Q 10 9 8 3 2	♠ A
♡ 8 3 2	♡ A K Q J 10 4
◇ —	◇ 9 8 6 3
♣ Q 10 3	♣ A 7

Opener bid 3 ♠, responder followed with a rather dubious raise to 4 ♠, and everyone passed! Responder's sketchy spade support does present a problem, but the good (and makable) grand slam might well have been reached as follows:

Opener	*Responder*
3 ♠	5 ◇ (a)
5 NT (b)	6 ♣ (c)
7 ♣ (d)	7 ♠ (e)
Pass	

(a) Control Asking Bid (4 ◇ would be natural and forcing).
(b) First-round control in diamonds.
(c) The Delayed Grand Slam Force.
(d) Two of the top three spade honors.
(e) Likely to be better than 7 ♡, since the spade suit may well be blocked.

Here's another example, this time from a 1970 National Tournament:

Opener		*Responder*	
♠	A K 10 7 6 5 4 2	♠	9
♡	4	♡	A K J 8 3
◇	10 8 6 5	◇	A K 4
♣	—	♣	Q J 4 2

Few players who held these hands had any idea how to bid them. Some closed their eyes and pushed to six; others stopped short of slam. Control Asking Bids make possible a knowledgeable approach:

Opener	*Responder*
4 ♠	5 ♣ (a)
5 ♠ (b)	6 ♠ (c)
Pass	

(a) Control Asking Bid.
(b) First-round control in clubs.
(c) There will probably be a spade loser—and that's all.
     Opener actually might make seven if spades· split 2-2
     and the heart suit can be ruffed out for an extra
     diamond pitch, but the grand slam is clearly a poor
     gamble.

Given that the Control Asking Bid agrees on opener's suit as
the trump suit, there may even be occasions when you can use two
asking bids in a single auction:

Opener		*Responder*	
♠	K J 10 8 7 5 3	♠	A Q 9 2
♡	3	♡	A Q 10 8 6 5 4
◇	8 5 4	◇	—
♣	A 2	♣	K 8

Opener	*Responder*
3 ♠ (or 4 ♠)	5 ♣ (a)
5 ♠ (b)	6 ♡ (c)
6 NT (d)	7 ♠
Pass	

(a) Control Asking Bid.
(b) First-round control in clubs.
(c) By partnership agreement, a second Control Asking
     Bid rather than an attempt to play in hearts. Responder

knows that he will not get too high, as opener will bid
6 ♠ if he lacks any controls in hearts.
(d) Second-round control of hearts.

Control Asking Bids are not much harder to use than Blackwood, and they are well worth the effort to learn them. They do
have one disadvantage, however: They inform the opponents where
your weak link is most likely to be, and make it probable that you'll
get the most damaging opening lead. At times, therefore, you'll do
better to bid slam directly. For example, suppose partner opens with
3 ♡ in first position, neither side vulnerable, and you hold:

> ♠ A
> ♡ J 10 3
> ◇ A 5 3
> ♣ A K Q 7 6 2

You probably have a heart loser, and may also lose a diamond
trick if the opponents lead the suit at once and drive out your ace
while retaining their trump trick as an entry. You could find out if
partner has a diamond control by using a Control Asking Bid, but a
direct jump to 6 ♡ should work out better. The opponents have
three suits to guess among when choosing their opening lead, and
they may well go wrong if you don't go out of your way to call their
attention to diamonds. And even if a diamond is led, a quick discard
on the top clubs could still save the day (and your slam).

The Major-Suit Trump Asking Bid. Another vexing situation
occurs when partner opens with 4 ♠, the next player passes, and
you hold a hand like:

> ♠ —
> ♡ A K 9 8 6 3
> ◇ A K 4 2
> ♣ A 5 3

The success of any slam venture depends on the strength of partner's suit, but the Grand Slam Force won't help you here. You don't even want to be in *six* spades if partner has:

     ♠ A Q 9 8 7 6 5 3
     ♡ 5
     ♢ 6 3
     ♣ 6 4

Therefore it's desirable to use the direct raise from 4 ♠ to 5 ♠, or from 4 ♡ to 5 ♡, to ask partner to go on to slam *if his suit has at most one loser.* This Trump Asking Bid guarantees first-round control (ace or void) in every side suit, and also ensures that there will be enough tricks for slam so long as a disaster in the trump suit can be avoided. With the hand shown above, opener will pass; with either of the following hands, he will go on to 6 ♠:

(a) ♠ K Q J 10 7 6 3 2   (b) ♠ A Q J 9 8 7 6 5
      ♡ 7 2   ♡ 4
      ♢ 5   ♢ 6 3
      ♣ 6 4   ♣ 6 4

The spade suit in hand (a) will undoubtedly lose only one trick even opposite a void, while the spades in hand (b) have an excellent chance of suffering just one loser (any 3-2 split, or a singleton king or ten, will do). If instead opener happens to have a long suit headed by A K Q J, he can either bid the grand slam directly or, by partnership agreement, make an unusual response (such as six of a new suit) in case you were stretching a bit and want to stop at the six-level anyway.

The Trump Asking Bid gives up fairly little since you will rarely want to use the single raise of partner's 4 ♡ or 4 ♠ opening bid as an advance sacrifice. The auction is already at a very high level, and it would be catastrophic to go down one in a five-level contract when your side actually could have made game. This convention does *not* apply, however, if your right-hand opponent inserts a bid, since you may well wish to sacrifice in such a situation.

If partner opens with 3 ♡ or 3 ♠ and the next player passes, a raise to the five-level can be used either as the Trump Asking Bid or as an advance sacrifice. The latter procedure is more standard, so don't use this asking bid without a firm prior agreement with your partner. When your right-hand opponent bids or doubles, the jump raise is unquestionably an advance sacrifice.

Responding to a Weak Two-Bid

We have seen that a Weak Two-Bid is similar to a three-level preempt but shows one trick less, and frequently is based on only a six-card suit. A typical example would be:

$$
\begin{array}{ll}
♠ & A\ Q\ J\ 9\ 7\ 6 \\
♡ & 5\ 3 \\
◊ & 6\ 2 \\
♣ & 10\ 7\ 2
\end{array}
$$

Your strategy as responder remains basically similar, except that you need somewhat better support (and somewhat more strength) in order to get into the auction. Also, a new response of 2 NT is available, and it is used in a special (conventional) way by most adherents of Weak Two-Bids.

RAISES

Raises to game are two-way bids. If partner opens with 2 ♠ and you raise to 4 ♠, you may simply be bidding what you expect to make with a hand like:

$$
\begin{array}{lll}
\text{(a)} & ♠ & K\ 10\ 4 \\
& ♡ & A\ K\ 7\ 5 \\
& ◊ & 9\ 8 \\
& ♣ & A\ Q\ J\ 3
\end{array}
$$

Alternatively, your 4 ♠ response may actually be an advance sacrifice with a holding like:

$$
\begin{aligned}
\text{(b)} \quad &♠ \quad \text{K 10 4 3} \\
&♡ \quad 2 \\
&♢ \quad \text{A 9 7 5 3} \\
&♣ \quad \text{J 8 5}
\end{aligned}
$$

This enables you to put a great deal of pressure on your opponents. If they guess wrong and enter the auction when you have hand (a), they are likely to suffer a disastrous penalty; if they discreetly pass and find you with hand (b), they'll miss a cold game. And your tactics are safe from interference by your partner, since he must pass your raise.

Single raises are mild preempts, and partner is again expected to pass. For example, suppose that both sides are vulnerable, partner opens with 2♡, and you hold:

$$
\begin{aligned}
&♠ \quad \text{Q 3 2} \\
&♡ \quad \text{A J 6} \\
&♢ \quad \text{10 9 7 6 5} \\
&♣ \quad \text{6 5}
\end{aligned}
$$

You would like to cooperate with partner's preemptive tactics in view of your meager defensive strength, but a high-level contract could easily go down 800 or 1100 (or more) against the opponents' 600-point game. Therefore a raise to 3 ♡ is a reasonable choice.

Here again, you can keep the opponents off-balance by raising partner's 2 ♡ opening bid to 3♡ with a hand like:

$$
\begin{aligned}
&♠ \quad \text{A J 9 8} \\
&♡ \quad \text{Q 4} \\
&♢ \quad \text{A J 9 6 3} \\
&♣ \quad \text{10 7}
\end{aligned}
$$

A three-level contract should be safe in view of your aces and partner's promised six-card heart suit. If the opponents blithely enter the auction in the belief that you are pitifully weak, they may well be in for a most unpleasant surprise.

NEW-SUIT RESPONSES

New-suit responses to a Weak Two-Bid are generally played as forcing. Opener is expected to raise a major-suit response if he has decent support (three cards or more, or perhaps even a doubleton honor). Otherwise, he may bid notrump to suggest that his suit is likely to run, cue-bid a side-suit high card if he can do so cheaply and has a maximum hand, or return to his original suit. Jumps to game in a new suit are signoffs.

A fair number of players prefer to use non-jump new-suit responses as signoffs. This approach may sometimes achieve a rescue in the nick of time, but it tends to crowd the bidding too much when responder has a good hand, and tends to preempt the opponents too little when responder has a long and strong suit of his own and few defensive values. It is moderately popular, however, so check out this issue with your partner before sitting down to play.

NOTRUMP RESPONSES

The only important new feature occasioned by partner's Weak Two-Bid is the 2 NT response, which is forcing and requests more information about opener's hand. Different players use this bid in different ways, and the most common alternatives are:

"Mini-Maxi" Rebids. Opener answers the 2 NT response as follows:

> 3 ♣ = poor hand, poor suit
> 3 ◇ = poor hand, good suit
> 3 ♡ = good hand, poor suit
> 3 ♠ = good hand, good suit

(Some players reverse the meanings of the 3 ◇ and 3 ♡ bids.)

This method has the advantage of giving information about two important aspects of opener's hand—his overall strength and the strength of his long suit.

Feature Rebids. Using this method, opener replies to 2 NT by showing a side-suit honor if he has one. Otherwise he returns to three of his suit. The advantage of this approach is that responder can often determine whether or not a crucial side suit is stopped for purposes of notrump play, since opener has shown where his outside high card is (or isn't). A possible disadvantage is that some difficulty may arise when opener's high card is in a suit above his original suit. For example, if opener bids 2 ♡ and responder bids 2 NT, opener can show an honor in clubs or diamonds quite cheaply; but if he has an important spade stopper and a borderline hand, a 3 ♠ bid may get his side too high.

Singleton Rebids. Some players use the 2 NT response to inquire about the possibility of a singleton in opener's hand. If he has one, he bids it; otherwise he returns to three of his suit. Singletons can be quite important for slam purposes (as we will see in Chapter 5, when "Splinter Bids" will be discussed), and this method has the advantage of locating any at a low level of bidding.

The McCabe Adjunct. Some players who treat new-suit responses to Weak Two-Bids as forcing use a device called the McCabe Adjunct (named after its inventor, J. I. McCabe) when they wish to escape to a different suit. It works as follows: A 2 NT response compels opener to rebid 3 ♣ regardless of his hand. If responder now bids a new suit, opener must pass; if responder wants to play in clubs, he simply passes 3 ♣.

Responding to a Preemptive Overcall

The procedures for responding to an opening preempt can be used pretty much intact for purposes of responding to a preemptive overcall. The only new possibility concerns a cue-bid of the enemy suit. If this occurs below the level of 3 NT (as could happen after a Weak Jump Overcall), partner is asked to bid game in notrump if he has a stopper in the opponents' suit. At higher levels, the cue-bid can either be a general slam try asking partner to show a side-suit king or ace if he had one, or (by partnership agreement) a Control

Asking Bid inquiring about partner's ability to prevent the loss of two tricks in the enemy suit.

When responding to a preemptive overcall, keep in mind that it will be easier for the opponents to double you because of the information provided by their opening bid. Somewhat more conservatism may therefore be desirable.

Penalty Doubles

On some happy occasions, partner's preempt will goad the opponents into a foolhardy course of action. Be careful, however, not to inflict the disaster on your side:

(a)	♠	K Q 3	(b)	♠	A J 9 7
	♡	7 2		♡	3
	◊	A 6 4 3		◊	K Q 10 6
	♣	5 4 3 2		♣	A K J 2

If partner deals and opens with 4 ♡, both sides vulnerable, and your right-hand opponent overcalls with 4 ♠, you should pass with hand (a). Partner may well have no defensive tricks at all, and your left-hand opponent just might be about to fall victim to the pressure provided by partner's preempt and raise to a contract that you can surely defeat. With hand (b), however, you should double. Your opponent is clearly in serious trouble, so cash in on his blunder by making him pay the full penalty.

Review Quiz

In each of the following problems, the vulnerability and bidding are shown. What call do you make?

(1) Both sides vulnerable

YOU	LHO	PARTNER	RHO	You hold:
—	—	3 ♡	Pass	♠ A K 6
?				♡ 9
				◇ A 10 5 3 2
				♣ K Q 4 3

(2) Opponents are vulnerable

YOU	LHO	PARTNER	RHO	You hold:
—	—	3 ♠	Double	♠ J 9 7 6
?				♡ 5
				◇ A 6 4 3
				♣ A 5 4 2

(3) Both sides vulnerable

YOU	LHO	PARTNER	RHO	You hold:
—	—	3 ♠	Double	♠ J 9 7
?				♡ 5 2
				◇ A 6 4 3
				♣ J 10 9 8

(4) In Problems 2 and 3, would your answers be different if your right-hand opponent had overcalled 4 ♡?

(5) Neither side vulnerable

YOU	LHO	PARTNER	RHO	You hold:
—	—	4 ♡	Pass	♠ A 9 8 4
?				♡ 10 8 7
				◇ A 3 2
				♣ A 8 3

(6) Neither side vulnerable

YOU	LHO	PARTNER	RHO	You hold:
—	—	3 ♡	Pass	♠ Q J 6 3
?				♡ 8
				◇ K Q J 6
				♣ K Q 5 4

(7) Both sides vulnerable

YOU	LHO	PARTNER	RHO	You hold:
Pass	Pass	3 ♠	4 ♡	♠ J 6
?				♡ 9 7 4 3
				◇ A K 10 6
				♣ Q 8 6

(8) Neither side vulnerable

YOU	LHO	PARTNER	RHO	You hold:
—	Pass	3 ◇	Pass	♠ A Q 9 7 4 3
?				♡ A K 3
				◇ 6
				♣ A 10 2

(9) Opponents are vulnerable

YOU	LHO	PARTNER	RHO	You hold:
—	—	3 ♠	Pass	♠ A 6 5
?				♡ Q J 10 9
				◊ K Q J
				♣ K Q 10

(10) Both sides vulnerable

YOU	LHO	PARTNER	RHO	You hold:
—	—	3 ♣	Pass	♠ A 7 6
?				♡ Q J 10 9
				◊ A 7 5
				♣ A 6 4

(11) Opponents are vulnerable

YOU	LHO	PARTNER	RHO	You hold:
—	1 ♣	3 ♠	4 ♡	♠ Q 8 6 4
?				♡ 3
				◊ A K 3 2
				♣ 7 6 5 3

(12) Opponents are vulnerable

YOU	LHO	PARTNER	RHO	You hold:
—	—	2 ♠*	Pass	♠ K Q 7 6
?				♡ A K 9 7 5
	*Weak Two-Bid			◊ 3 2
				♣ A 4

(13) Opponents are vulnerable

YOU	LHO	PARTNER	RHO	You hold:
—	—	2 ♡*	Pass	♠ 7 3
?				♡ Q 8 6 2
		*Weak Two-Bid		♦ A J 10 4 3
				♣ 9 8

(14) Neither side vulnerable

YOU	LHO	PARTNER	RHO	You hold:
—	1 ♡	2 ♠*	3 ♡	♠ Q 8 6 5
?				♡ A 3
		*Weak Jump Overcall		♦ A 8 6 4 3
				♣ 3 2

(15) Opponents are vulnerable

YOU	LHO	PARTNER	RHO	You hold:
Pass	1 ♠	3 ♦*	6 ♠	♠ A 7 3
?				♡ 7
		*Weak Jump Overcall		♦ Q 8 7 6 5
				♣ 8 6 4 3

(16) Both sides vulnerable

YOU	LHO	PARTNER	RHO	You hold:
—	—	4 ♣	4 ♠	♠ K J 9
?				♡ A 6 4 2
				♦ Q 7 5
				♣ 6 3 2

(17) Both sides vulnerable

YOU	LHO	PARTNER	RHO	You hold:
—	—	4 ◇	4 ♠	♠ Q J 9 7 6
?				♡ 5
				◇ J 9 7 6
				♣ A 4 3

(18) Both sides vulnerable

YOU	LHO	PARTNER	RHO	You hold:
—	—	4 ♣	4 ♡	♠ A K 9 7
?				♡ Q 8 6
				◇ A K 6 5
				♣ 10 9

(19) Opponents are vulnerable

YOU	LHO	PARTNER	RHO	You hold:
—	1 ♠	4 ♣	4 ♠	♠ K 4
?				♡ A Q J 9 5 3
				◇ K 8 7 5
				♣ Q

(20) Both sides vulnerable

YOU	LHO	PARTNER	RHO	You hold:
—	—	5 ♣	Pass	♠ A K 7 6 3
?				♡ A K 4 3 2
				◇ A 5 4
				♣ —

(21) Both sides vulnerable

YOU	LHO	PARTNER	RHO	You hold:
—	—	4 ♠	Pass	♠ —
?				♡ A 5 4
				◇ A K J 6 3
				♣ A K Q 3 2

(22) Both sides vulnerable

YOU	LHO	PARTNER	RHO	You hold:
—	—	3 ♠	Pass	♠ A J 7 6 2
?				♡ A K
				◇ Q J 6 3
				♣ A K

(23) Neither side vulnerable

YOU	LHO	PARTNER	RHO	You hold:
—	—	4 ♡	Pass	♠ A K 2
?				♡ Q 8 4
				◇ A K J 9 7 6 4
				♣ —

(24) Both sides vulnerable

YOU	LHO	PARTNER	RHO	You hold:
—	—	4 ♡	Pass	♠ A K 4 3 2
?				♡ A
				◇ A K J 9 7
				♣ K Q

(25) Both sides vulnerable

YOU	LHO	PARTNER	RHO	You hold:
3 ♣	Pass	3 ♡	Pass	♠ 4 3
?				♡ K 7
				◇ 3 2
				♣ A Q 10 9 7 6 4

Solutions

1. *Four hearts.* Partner's vulnerable three-bid promises six or seven tricks and you can add four more, so game should be there for the taking. Avoid notrump with a poor fit for partner's suit; you'll probably get cut off from his hand in the likely event that he lacks a side-suit entry. Partner's hand:

♠ 5 2
♡ A Q J 8 7 6 4
◇ 8 4
♣ 6 2

2. *Five spades.* Your vulnerable opponents should be cold for game in hearts, so make your maximum preempt at once. Partner is unlikely to have any defensive tricks in view of your spade length, so a 5 ♠ sacrifice should be an excel-

lent investment; the opponents may well succumb to the pressure and push on to a hopeless slam. A 4 ♠ bid might save you 200 points on occasion, but it is too likely to give the opponents the extra bidding room that will enable them to reach the right decision.

3. *Four spades*. The opponents can make a lot, but the vulnerability and your weak hand make a high-level preempt too dangerous. You can afford a single raise, however, so hope that this will be just enough to disrupt the opponents' bidding.

4. *No*. The previous answers remain correct.

5. *Pass*. Partner's bid shows about six or seven tricks, so slam is clearly out of reach.

6. *Pass*. Hands like this illustrate the disadvantage of preempting. The opponents probably can't make a thing in view of your defensive strength, and you could easily incur an appreciable penalty because your hand fits poorly with partner. Don't make things even worse by bidding because you have a fair number of points; side-suit queens and jacks don't figure to be worth a great deal opposite a preempt. Partner's hand:

♠ 5 4
♡ K Q 10 7 6 5 4
◇ 3
♣ 7 6 2

7. *Four spades*. You don't rate to beat 4 ♡ opposite a partner who is lacking in defensive strength, so give the opponents a gentle push in the wrong direction. If they think that you are raising with super spade support and meager defensive values, they are likely to make the wrong decision—as actually happened when this deal was played in the 1969 World Championships:

```
                          NORTH
                          ♠  10 5
                          ♡  K Q J 10 8 6 5
                          ◇  Q
                          ♣  A 4 3
WEST (partner)                                EAST (you)
♠  A K 9 8 7 4 2                              ♠  J 6
♡  2                                          ♡  9 7 4 3
◇  8 5 4 2                                    ◇  A K 10 6
♣  2                                          ♣  Q 8 6
                          SOUTH
                          ♠  Q 3
                          ♡  A
                          ◇  J 9 7 3
                          ♣  K J 10 9 7 5
```

The bidding:

SOUTH	WEST	NORTH	EAST
—	—	—	Pass
Pass	3 ♠	4 ♡	4 ♠
5 ♣	Pass	Pass	Pass

South lost the obvious three tricks and went down one, while 4 ♡ would have made easily. (North gives up his three losers and runs all the hearts, and East must blank his club queen—and spare declarer any chance of a misguess—in order to protect against South's jack of diamonds.) And even if North and South had elected to defend, 4 ♠ would have gone down only one trick.

8. *Three spades*. Major-suit games require one less trick than minor-suit games, so you are justified in seeking support for your long suit. Partner is requested to raise with three small spades or better, or with a doubleton honor. If he

returns to 4 ◇ , you can hazard a shot at 5 ◇ , as he should have a respectable suit to preempt in second position.

9. *Three notrump.* There could easily be four top losers in a 4 ♠ contract, and your spade fit should ensure sufficient access to partner's long suit.

10. *Three notrump.* If partner's vulnerable preempts are reasonably trustworthy, nine tricks are likely to be there for the taking. His hand actually is:

> ♠ 5 2
> ♡ 4 2
> ◇ 6 3
> ♣ K Q J 9 7 5 3

Players addicted to light preempts are likely to have trouble in situations like this. Responder cannot be sure when to bid 3 NT, since opener's suit is an unknown quantity. And if opener runs from notrump because his suit is weak, he may find to his sorrow that responder had a solid minor of his own and that 3 NT was the only makable game.

11. *Five spades.* Take the advance sacrifice, just as you would in response to a preemptive opening bid. Your left-hand opponent is probably champing at the bit to show his heart support, and you will have a surprise for him if he does.

12. *Four spades.* Your strong hand and partner's strong spade suit should provide a good play for game.

13. *Four hearts.* This should be a fine sacrifice even if the opponents double, and you may steal the hand if they think you are raising on power.

14. *Four spades.* Partner's Weak Jump Overcall announces that his defensive values are quite limited, so even your two aces don't figure to be enough to defeat 4 ♡ . Therefore it's time for an advance sacrifice.

15. *Seven diamonds.* For a change, the opponents are trying to make *you* guess at a high level. Partner's Weak Jump Overcall has advised you that he can't be counted on for much in the way of defense, so the sacrifice is indicated. His hand:

♠   6
♥   9 8 3 2
♦   K J 10 9 4 3
♣   J 10

16. *Pass.* Partner could easily have no defensive tricks at all, so you are not strong enough to double.
17. *Pass.* The opponents have stumbled into what is likely to be the only contract you can defeat. Don't scare them into a makable one by doubling.
18. *Double.* This time, your right-hand opponent is clearly out of his depth, and it's time to reap the maximum profit.
19. *Pass.* A double is acceptable also. The important thing is that your distribution and high cards argue against a sacrifice. Here's the complete deal, which arose in the 1958 World Championships:

NORTH
♠   J 9 8 6 5 3
♥   K 6 2
♦   Q J 9
♣   7

WEST (partner)
♠   10
♥   8
♦   6 4 2
♣   A J 8 6 5 4 3 2

EAST (you)
♠   K 4
♥   A Q J 9 5 3
♦   K 8 7 5
♣   Q

SOUTH
♠   A Q 7 2
♥   10 7 4
♦   A 10 3
♣   K 10 9

The 4 ♠ contract goes down; the defenders can beat it two tricks by leading a heart and cashing two heart tricks, giving West a heart ruff, and cashing the club ace and playing another club to enable East to score his king of trumps via an overruff. The actual East player, however, bid 5 ♣—and suffered a penalty of 500 points.

20. *Six clubs.* Partner's suit is likely to have only one loser in view of the vulnerability, and no good conventional bid is available.

21. *Five spades (Trump Asking Bid).* Partner will pass if his spade suit has two losers, bid 6 ♠ if it has only one loser, and do something spectacular (such as bidding 7 ♠ or six of a new suit) if his spades are headed by A K Q J. Players not using this convention must close their eyes, bid 6 ♠, and hope for the best.

22. *Five diamonds (Control Asking Bid).* The Control Asking Bid enables you to find out whether or not the opponents can take the first two tricks in diamonds. If partner answers 5 ♡ (first step), you have two diamond losers and should stop in 5 ♠. If he bids 5 ♠ (second step), showing the diamond king or a singleton diamond, you can safely bid 6 ♠. And if he bids 5 NT, promising first-round control of diamonds (ace or void), you should bid 7 ♠.

23. *Five notrump (Direct Grand Slam Force).* If partner bids 6 ♡, showing one of the top three heart honors, you will pass. If he has the ace and king of hearts, he will bid 7 ♣ and you will correct to 7 ♡. Blackwood is ill-advised in this situation, for it won't tell you whether partner's high honors are in hearts or clubs.

24. *Four notrump (Blackwood).* If partner has no aces, risk 6 ♡; there might be a heart loser, but the odds are against it (and there is no safe way to find out for sure). If partner does have the ace of clubs, however, no guesswork will be necessary. Bid 6 ♣ (the Delayed Grand Slam Force); partner will bid 6 ♡ if the king or queen of hearts is missing (and you will pass), and will bid 7 ♣ with both of the top hearts (and you will bid 7 ♡).

25. *Four hearts.* Partner's new-suit response asks for support with the slightest excuse. He already knows about your long clubs.

4

Overcoming Enemy Preempts

♠ ♡ ◇ ♣

Now that we have examined the fundamental principles of preemptive bidding, it's time to see what can be done when your devilish opponents attempt to turn the tables on you. Overcoming a preempt is a murky area even among experts, and such otherwise comprehensive tomes as *The Official Encyclopedia of Bridge* and *Goren's Bridge Complete* devote only about one page to this difficult topic. Since there is no single ideal defensive procedure, this chapter will concentrate on some helpful hints that improve your chances of surviving the enemy bidding barrage.

Doubles of Preemptive Opening Bids

There are several different ways of using the double of an opening three-bid or four-bid by your right-hand opponent,* and most of these methods have some merit. We'll consider each one in turn.

PENALTY DOUBLES

Penalty doubles announce that the opponents are in terrible trouble, and virtually order partner to pass unless he has very freakish distribution. It's tempting to use penalty doubles so that you can collect a bundle when you are lucky enough to hold three or four trump tricks and several high cards on the side. Unfortunately,

---

*Except for the double of a 4 ♠ opening, which (as we will see later in this chapter) is a special case.

the double is more likely to be needed for other purposes, so this procedure is of dubious value at best. However, if your opponents are known to be addicted to light preempts, you may do well by using penalty doubles against them—provided that you and your partner agree upon an alternative procedure for coping with situations like:

<pre>
             RHO opens 3 ♡
             ♠ A 6 4 3
             ♡ 7
             ◇ A K 4 2
             ♣ K J 10 5
</pre>

None of your suits is strong enough for an overcall, so you need some way of asking partner to bid his best suit. One formerly popular method used an overcall in the next higher suit (for example, a 3 ♠ overcall of a 3 ♡ opening bid) as an artificial bid, asking partner to take out to his best suit (the *Fishbein Convention*). However, this approach cannot be recommended (and is no longer widely used) because the major-suit overcall is likely to be needed as a natural bid. Another possibility is to use the 3 NT overcall as a conventional demand to partner to bid his best suit, but this also uses up a bid that might well be needed for natural purposes. A third procedure, and perhaps the best one, is to use the overcall in the *cheaper minor* (for example, 4 ♣ over a 3 ♡ preempt, 3 ◇ over a 3 ♣ preempt, and so on) to order partner to remove to his best suit. This preserves the natural meaning of the important major-suit and notrump overcalls, although problems will arise on those occasions when you need the overcall in the cheaper minor suit as a natural bid.

INFORMATORY DOUBLES

Informatory doubles allow partner some leeway. They tell him that you have a strong and relatively balanced hand (about 16 points or more), but they do *not* guarantee support for all unbid suits. Therefore he may bid with a long and strong suit of his own, or with two respectable suits that give him two chances to find a good resting place; but he should pass with an undistinguished balanced hand, even if he has a four-card major suit. For example, an informatory double of a 3 ♡ opening bid would be made with either of these hands:

(a) (Deal 1)   (b) ♠ K 6 4
     ♠ A 6   ♡ 4 3 2
     ♡ 6 4 3 2   ◇ A K Q
     ◇ A K 7 3   ♣ A 9 7 6
     ♣ A Q 4

This approach is a lifesaver in either case, since it enables you to show your considerable strength without risking a disastrous spade response by partner on four to the queen. It can reasonably be argued, however, that locating a major-suit fit is of extreme importance. Therefore an acceptable modification is to play that informatory doubles of a *major*-suit preempt *do* promise support for the other major. This works poorly in the above examples, but is ideal when you hold something like:

(c) ♠ K Q 7 6
     ♡ 9 6 3
     ◇ A 7
     ♣ A K J 5

You'll be happy to double a 3 ♡ preempt under the agreement that partner will bid a four-card spade suit, but not a four-card minor.

OPTIONAL DOUBLES

Optional doubles emphasize takeout rather than penalties. They show about 16 points or more, and ask partner to bid a four-card or longer suit. He may pass for penalties, however, if his hand is so shapeless and mediocre that any bid is likely to result in disaster (or, of course, if he is loaded in the enemy suit). For example, if your right-hand opponent opens with 3 $\diamondsuit$, an optional double would show a hand such as:

♠   J 10 9 3
♡   A K 5 3
♢   A 7
♣   K Q 9

You definitely want partner to bid a four-card major and can tolerate a club response. And if he passes because he cannot find a sensible bid, your defensive strength should be enough to defeat the enemy contract.

"Optional doubles" are in widespread use among today's experts. However, this is partly because this term is so vague that a player can call almost anything an "optional double" and then blame his partner for making the wrong decision. For example, most optional doublers *would* double with hands (a), (b), and (c) in the preceding section, even though they would be in serious trouble if partner bid spades opposite hand (a) or responded in diamonds opposite hand (c) or bid a mediocre four-card spade or diamond suit opposite hand (b). Consequently, there is much to be said in favor of informatory doubles. Although they may miss some good 4-4 fits, they will at least provide some income in the form of a doubled penalty, while off-shape optional doubles are likely to end up with a minus score instead of the plus that Fate (and your many high cards) had intended. And informatory doubles have an extra advantage: When partner does bid over them, he must have a pretty good offensive hand. Therefore he doesn't have to jump the bidding (and risk getting too high if you had a marginal double) just to show you that he has some useful values.

TAKEOUT DOUBLES

A final choice (and the one recommended by Goren) is to use the double of a three-bid to insist that partner take out to his best suit, just as you would over the opening bid of one of a suit. The takeout double shows about 16 points or more and guarantees fine support for all unbid suits. Thus partner may pass only if he has a trump stack and strongly wishes to play for the penalty. Otherwise he must bid his best suit, even a three-carder. A typical minimum takeout double of a 3 ◊ preempt would be:

♠ A 9 7 5
♡ K J 6 2
◊ 4
♣ A Q 8 7

Doubles of four-level or five-level preempts may be passed, however, as the doubler surely has enough strength to defeat such high-level contracts. Thus these doubles are optional rather than unilateral takeouts.

Takeout doubles do gain when ideal hands like the one above come up; informatory and optional doublers also must double, and their partners are more likely to make an inopportune pass. However, it is by no means clear that takeout doubles are as desirable as their advocates suggest. Unlike an opening one-bid, a preempt is very likely to end the auction because it discourages the preempter's partner from pushing on with marginal values. Also, you are much more likely to want to penalize a preempt than a one-bid. Therefore you simply can't afford to sit back and wait with a powerful hand just because you don't happen to have good support for one of the unbid suits. In fact, even confirmed takeout doublers would probably double with hands (a), (b), and (c) that we looked at awhile back. This may indicate that most experts haven't given enough thought to the best way to use the double of an opening preempt; or it may imply that getting to the right spot after an enemy preempt is at best a mad scramble requiring considerable luck, and that attempting to define the double very precisely is an impossible undertaking.

THE WAITING PASS

In view of the controversial nature of doubles of opening preempts, it's up to you and your favorite partner(s) to decide whether you prefer informatory, optional, or takeout doubles before you sit down to play. But these three methods do agree with regard to one particular strategy. Suppose your right-hand opponent opens with 3 ◇ or 4 ◇ and you hold:

> ♠ 7 6
> ♡ A K 2
> ◇ K Q 10 8
> ♣ J 10 9 7

You are almost certain to defeat the enemy contract, but a double could easily elicit a fatal bid from your partner. Therefore you must pass. Partner may reopen with a double, enabling you to pass for penalties. And even if he passes, it's better to collect an undoubled penalty than to get to some silly contract and pay out a lot of points.

Doubles of Weak Two-Bids

Matters are much simpler after an enemy Weak Two-Bid, and relatively standard methods should suffice. Takeout doubles are preferable, since you don't want partner to risk a doubtful pass when the opponents need only eight tricks to bring home their contract. However, you do need somewhat more strength to double a Weak Two-Bid than a one-bid; a very good 14 points or more should be enough.

With a balanced hand worth a strong notrump opening bid and the enemy suit well stopped, a 2 NT overcall is likely to work out better than a double. Similarly, a 3 NT overcall is also natural; it may be made with an even stronger balanced hand, or with a long and solid minor suit plus stoppers in the opponents' suit.

Overcalls of Preemptive Opening Bids

SUIT OVERCALLS

If the enemy preempt finds you with a long, strong suit and a good hand (about 16 points or more), it's desirable to overcall in order to take the pressure off your partner. For example:

$$
\begin{array}{ll}
\spadesuit & \text{A 10 3} \\
\heartsuit & \text{A K 10 9 8 5} \\
\diamondsuit & \text{K J 10} \\
\clubsuit & \text{3}
\end{array}
$$

Your side is vulnerable, and you are enjoying pleasant day-dreams about opening the bidding when a rude awakening occurs: Your right-hand opponent, who has dealt, starts off with 4 ♣. Your best bet is to overcall with 4 ♡. You might be doubled and set, but you cannot afford to let the preempt terrorize you into submission when you have this much strength. To be sure, an optional or takeout double might enable partner to bid a long spade or diamond suit and get you to the right spot when he is short in hearts, but the double is far too likely to present him with an insoluble problem. He can't know that even a doubleton heart will be enough for a playable trump suit. Therefore he may well bid a four-card spade suit, or jump in diamonds, and get you to the wrong spot. Or he may pass and collect a small penalty when you are cold for game or even slam in hearts. A good guideline to remember is that when you have very little room to explore for the *best* contract, settle for what is likely to be a *good* one—here, by trotting out your long suit.

With a weak suit, discretion (and a pass) will often be the better part of valor. Even in such cases, however, an overcall may be your best choice:

♠ A 8 7 6 3
♡ 8 6 4
♢ A 3
♣ A K J

If both sides are vulnerable and your right-hand opponent deals and opens with 3 ♡, your first inclination probably will be to regret that the fiend ever learned anything about preemptive bidding. Your second thought, however, will be to enter the auction in view of your substantial strength, and the best way to do so is a 3 ♠ overcall. If you double, you won't have any idea whether or not to convert a minor-suit response to spades; partner could have a healthy six-card minor and a singleton or void in spades, or a sketchy five-card minor and three spades to an honor. The spade overall is risky because your suit is weak, but at least it gives you a fighting chance to reap some dividends from your venture into the auction. It will enable partner to raise with three-card spade support and about 10 points, thereby reaching your most likely game contract.

In some situations where there is no good solution, an overcall may be the least of evils:

♠ A Q 9 6
♡ K 4 3
♢ —
♣ K J 10 5 3 2

Your side is vulnerable, and your right-hand opponent deals and opens with 3 ♡. Just about any action could be right—or catastrophic. A pass will keep you out of trouble, but is likely to miss a good game or slam. A double might locate a valuable spade fit, but could easily bring forth a disastrous diamond response. Even a bizarre spade overcall, shocking as it is with only a four-card suit, could conceivably strike oil. However, the least unsatisfactory choice is a 4 ♣ overcall. It might lose a good spade fit, but at least it gets you into the fight and aims for what is reasonably likely to be a makable game contract. Whatever you choose, don't be too surprised if you wind up congratulating the opponents on the effectiveness of their preempt when the deal is over!*

Although suit overcalls are very useful, they can be overdone. The following hand requires a different strategy:

♠ K Q 8 6
♡ A K Q 5 3
♢ A 6 3
♣ 2

If your right-hand opponent opens with 3 ♣, an optional or takeout double or a cue-bid is preferable to a heart overcall. You very much want to hear about a four-card or longer spade suit in partner's hand, and you are strong enough to bid hearts next time if he happens to respond in diamonds.

THE 3 NT OVERCALL

A 3 NT overcall of a three-level preempt is natural, showing a balanced hand worth about 17-20 points, with the enemy suit well stopped. For example, if your right-hand opponent opens with 3 ♡, overcall 3 NT holding:

♠ K 8
♡ K Q 10
♢ A Q 9 2
♣ A J 10 7

The 3 NT overcall may also be made with a long and solid minor, since the nine-trick game may be much easier than trying to

*Because of problems like this, some experts play that a 4♣ or 4 ♢ overcall of a *major*-suit preempt shows the bid suit plus support for the unbid major. With a one-suited hand, they jump to five of their long minor. This interesting approach has not yet been used widely enough to permit adequate evaluation.

make five of your minor. However, be sure that you have a good hand with stoppers in the opponents' suit.

CUE-BIDS AND 4 NT OVERCALLS

On occasion a cue-bid of the enemy suit may be superior to a double. If your side is vulnerable and your right-hand opponent starts off with 3 ♡, cue-bid 4 ♡ with:

♠ K Q J 8
♡ —
◊ K Q 9 8
♣ A Q J 8 7

The cue-bid normally shows an extremely powerful three-suited hand. You are too strong offensively to double, for partner is likely to pass and limit your side to a trivial penalty when you are cold for game or slam.

A cue-bid can also be used when you hold the two *higher-*ranking unbid suits:

♠ A K 9 6 5 2
♡ —
◊ A K 9 7 6 5
♣ 4

Your side is vulnerable, and your right-hand opponent deals and opens with 4 ♡. In view of the severe shortage of bidding room, you may as well gamble that you belong in slam and cue-bid 5 ♡. If partner bids 6 ♣, as is likely, you will convert to 6 ◊ to inform him that you really want a choice between diamonds and spades.

Over a 4 ♠ opening bid, it is better to use the 4NT overcall to show a three-suited hand like:

♠ —
♡ A Q 6 5
◊ K Q 8 6 5
♣ K J 9 7

This enables you to play at the five-level when partner is weak, whereas a 5 ♠ cue-bid would force your side to slam. In addition, this approach allows you to use a double of a 4 ♠ opening bid primarily for penalties regardless of what doubling method you and your partner have selected.

After a 3 ♡, 3 ♠, or 4 ♡ preempt, a 4 NT overcall may be used to ask partner to take out to one of the *minor* suits. The reason for changing the strategy in these cases is that the 4 NT bid bypasses the level of four of the unbid major, so you can't afford it unless you are only interested in the minors. A typical 4 NT overcall of a 4 ♡ preempt would be:

♠ 7 3
♡ 6
◊ A K 10 7 6
♣ A K J 5 2

Since you are bypassing 4 ♠, partner is expected to restrict his selection to the minor suits.

Although the 4 NT overcalls described here are relatively standard, there are two alternative approaches that have some merit. One is to use the 4 NT overcall of a three-level preempt as a natural bid, showing a hand too strong for a mere 3 NT overcall (thus one worth about 21-24 points). This approach can be very helpful when the right hand comes up (see Deal 12), but opportunities to use it rarely occur. A second possibility is to use all 4 NT overcalls to show *any two* long suits. Responder bids his cheapest respectable suit, and the overcaller corrects if responder has hit his short suit. This method works well when right-hand opponent opens with 4 ♠ and you hold something like:

♠ 3
♡ K 7
◇ A Q 10 6 3
♣ A Q J 8 5

The best you can do using standard methods is to double, since you can't afford to risk a heart response to a 4 NT overcall (and since the double of a 4 ♠ opening bid is for penalties). The two-suited approach, however, allows you to overcall with 4 NT, since partner must not bid hearts unless he absolutely cannot stand either minor. The two-suited 4 NT overcall also applies if the hearts and diamonds are switched; partner must bid a decent club suit if he has one even if a higher-ranking suit is better, and you will convert a 5 ◇ response to 5 ♡. This procedure can lead to some confusion about the best trump suit, however, and currently is not standard practice.

There is little general agreement as to the meaning of 4 NT overcalls of *minor*-suit preempts. They can be used as Blackwood, as a takeout for the two lower-ranking unbid suits, or as natural bids. Here, as elsewhere, it's advisable to discuss your defensive procedures with your partner in advance.

The "Two Trick Rule" and Jump Suit Overcalls

All too often, enemy preempts push a partnership too high because one player makes a borderline but reasonable overcall or double, and the other player feels compelled to raise or jump the bidding because he has a couple of high cards that his partner may not have expected. (See Deals 2 and 13.) Here's a useful hint that will help avoid such disasters: *When partner enters the auction after an enemy preempt, discount your first two tricks (or your first 6-8 points).* Assume that partner has gambled on finding you with at least this much, and don't take aggressive action unless you have even more. For example:

(Deal 13)
♠ A 5 4
♡ A J 5
◊ 9 6 4
♣ J 8 5 2

The bidding (both sides vulnerable):

YOU	OPPONENT	PARTNER	OPPONENT
—	—	—	Pass
Pass	3 ◊	3 ♠	Pass
?			

It is understandable that the player who actually held these cards didn't feel like hanging a trick short of game, but the "Two Trick Rule" would have enabled him to find the winning pass. Under the assumption that partner is gambling on finding you with at least two tricks (or about 6-8 points), ignore your two aces. This leaves you with only two jacks and dismal distribution, which is not enough for a raise to game.

Another example:

(Deal 2)
♠ 8 6 3
♡ 8 3 2
◊ K Q J 8 7 4
♣ J

The bidding (neither side vulnerable):

YOU	OPPONENT	PARTNER	OPPONENT
—	4 ♣	Double	Pass
?			

Overly impressed by his strong suit, the player who held these cards jumped to 5 ♢—and got destroyed. The "Two Trick Rule" would point the way to the superior 4 ♢ response, since there is little left to brag about after the first two tricks (or 6-8 points) are discounted. A good game would be unlikely to be missed, as pulling a four-level double shows a pretty good offensive hand in the first place and advises partner to go on if he has a very powerful hand. On the actual deal, a 4 ♢ bid would have saved at least 200 points and perhaps a lot more, since the opponents might have been afraid to double the diamond bidder into game.

Here's another illustration:

♠ J
♡ 8 6 5 4 3
♢ Q 9 4
♣ K 5 4 3

The bidding (your side vulnerable):

YOU	OPPONENT	PARTNER	OPPONENT
—	3 ♢	Double	Pass
?			

Deducting 6-8 points (or two tricks) leaves you with virtually nothing, so a 3 ♡ response is sufficient. Partner's hand is:

♠ A K Q 6 5
♡ A J 7 2
♢ 3
♣ A Q J

He will raise to 4 ♡ on the grounds that game should have some play even if you are very weak, and you'll be in the right spot.

If you misguidedly jump to 4 ♡ yourself, partner will almost surely make a slam try and get your side too high.

If partner doubles a very high-level preempt, you can always pass if you are in doubt because he must have enough strength to defeat the contract. Therefore a bid by you shows a good offensive hand, and the "Two Trick Rule" is particularly likely to be valuable:

♠ K 7 4 2
♡ Q J 8 7 3
♢ A 6 4
♣ 2

The bidding (your side vulnerable):

YOU	OPPONENT	PARTNER	OPPONENT
—	—	—	5 ♢
Pass	Pass	Double	Pass
?			

It would not be a horrible error to insist upon slam at this point, but a 5 ♡ response is likely to work out better. Pulling the double of a five-level preempt shows an interest in slam, and you don't have much in excess of the "Two Trick Rule." A more aggressive bid could easily punish partner for competing with a borderline but reasonable hand, and could turn a sure game for your side into a minus score.

The "Two Trick Rule" does have one disadvantage. It puts extra pressure on the overcaller, and hence risks getting your side too high, when he has an extremely powerful hand:

♠ A Q J 7 3
♡ 7 6
♢ A K 3
♣ K Q 2

If your right-hand opponent opens with 3 ♡ and your side is using the "Two Trick Rule," you must *not* overcall with 3 ♠. Partner would pass, and miss a cold game, with:

♠ K 6 2
♡ 8 5 2
◇ 5 4 2
♣ A 8 6 3

Therefore you must either jump to 4 ♠ or, if you are using takeout doubles, double first and then bid spades. In spite of this drawback, the "Two Trick Rule" is a good way of accurately gauging your partnership prospects in most cases and is recommended for your adoption.

Balancing

If an opening preempt by your *left*-hand opponent is passed around to you, compete with about a trick less than you would need in direct position (in other words, about 13 points). For example, if the player on your left opens with 3 ♡ and the next two players pass, double with:

♠ K 10 4 2
♡ 9 7
◇ A Q 10 5
♣ K 8 6

Alternatively, overcall the 3 ♡ preempt with 3 ♠ if you are in the balance position and hold:

♠ A Q 9 7 6
♡ 8 4
◇ Q 10 6 2
♣ A 7

Neither hand is strong enough for a bid in second seat, but here you should act in case partner had to pass the preempt with a respectable hand.

"Staying Fixed"

After an enemy preempt, resist the temptation to become an overbidder or a perfectionist. Since there is no guaranteed effective defense, you will at times have to concede a loss to your opponents' preemptive tactics. In the long run you'll come out well ahead by avoiding unsound overcalls and doubles. Also, don't create your own destruction by searching frantically and (foolishly) for the best contract:

(Deal 8)
♠ A Q 10
♡ A 9 8 7
◇ 9 4
♣ J 9 8 6

The bidding (your side vulnerable):

YOU	OPPONENT	PARTNER	OPPONENT
—	—	—	Pass
Pass	3 ♣	3 ◇	4 ♣
?			

You should double. If partner passes, the penalty may not equal the value of your vulnerable game, but it's better to take the sure plus than to fumble around for the right spot at the four-level. The player who actually held these cards tried for perfection by bidding 4 ♡, and wound up with a minus score when his partner elected to pass with a doubleton heart.

Here's a similar example:

```
        ♠ Q 4 3 2
        ♡ 4 3 2
        ◇ 9 8 7
        ♣ A 8 6
```

The bidding (your side vulnerable):

YOU	OPPONENT	PARTNER	OPPONENT
—	4 ◇	Double	Pass
?			

You might have game in spades, but trying for the ideal spot with such meager values and unenviable distribution is all too likely to get you in trouble. Your high cards plus partner's promised strength should easily defeat the opponents' contract. So "stay fixed," pass, and get some profit at least. In fact, you should even pass with:

```
        ♠ 7 4 3 2
        ♡ 4 3 2
        ◇ 9 8 7
        ♣ 9 8 6
```

It's better to gamble that partner can take four tricks than to concede what is almost certain to be a huge penalty by bidding something. Partner's hand:

♠ A K 8
♡ A J 6 5
◇ A 2
♣ Q J 10 7

Even if an untimely ruff enables the opponents to make 4 ◇ doubled, you'll lose only 510 points, whereas bidding would cost you around 1100. And there is every chance that 4 ◇ will be defeated, enabling you to escape with a small plus.

To be sure, settling for the sure plus will be very costly if your side is cold for slam. (See Deal 9.) In view of the difficulty of getting to the right spot after an enemy preempt, however, "staying fixed" will often be the only realistic way to salvage at least some points from an extremely difficult situation.

Miscellaneous Tactics

NOTRUMP VS. MINORS

Since game in notrump requires two tricks less than game in clubs or diamonds, a stopper in the opponents' suit may well be more significant than a long minor suit:

♠ 7 4 3
♡ 9 3
◇ K 10 7
♣ K Q J 6 3

If your left-hand opponent opens with 3 ◇, partner doubles, and the next player passes, and you decide to bid, you should bid 3 NT. The enemy preempt has forced you to guess, and your rela-

tively balanced hand and diamond honors make the notrump game a
better gamble than a club bid.

LOCATING THE TRUMP SUIT

As was the case with 4 NT overcalls, a 4 NT response to a
double of a preemptive opening bid can be used to avoid landing in
the wrong suit:

(a)	YOU	OPPONENT	PARTNER	OPPONENT
	—	4 ♡	Double	Pass
	4 NT			

(b)	YOU	OPPONENT	PARTNER	OPPONENT
	—	4 ♠	Double	Pass
	4 NT			

In auction (a), the 4 NT bid asks partner to select his better
minor suit. His double doesn't guarantee support for both minors,
and you don't want to risk guessing the wrong one at the five-level if
you have a hand like:

♠ 7 3
♡ 2
♢ Q J 8 6 5
♣ Q J 8 6 5

In auction (b), your 4 NT bid requests partner to take out to one
of the three unbid suits. Here's an interesting illustration:

♠ 9 6 4
♡ K Q 8 4 3
♢ 8
♣ A 8 6 4

Even though partner's double is for penalties, he is very unlikely to have a trump stack in view of your spade length. He probably has a strong hand with fairly short spades, but was unable to bid 4 NT because he is also short in one of the unbid suits. Therefore a good strategy is to respond 4 NT. If partner bids clubs or hearts, you will raise to six; if he bids 5 ◇, you will bid 5 ♡ to invite slam without getting overboard.

OVERCOMING A PREEMPTIVE OVERCALL

If partner opens with one of a suit and the next player preempts, most bids can retain the usual meaning. For example, new-suit bids below game are natural and forcing, a 3 NT bid is natural and non-forcing, and a 4 NT response is generally used as Blackwood. A cue-bid of the opponents' suit can be used to request further information about partner's hand:

♠ K 9 7 4 2
♡ A
◇ K 10
♣ K J 10 7 3

If your side is vulnerable, partner opens with 1 ◇, and your right-hand opponent chimes in with 4 ♡, a cue-bid of 5 ♡ is the best solution. Partner is urged to choose between the unbid suits if he can, although he may rebid diamonds with a long, strong suit. Bidding one of your long suits could backfire badly, for you just might happen to find partner with a doubleton in the one you select and four to the ace-queen in the other—and not enough strength to take another bid. At lower levels and by partnership agreement, negative doubles may be used to request a choice between the unbid suits.

Traditionally, the *jump* raise to five of partner's *major* suit asks him to go on to slam if he has first-round or second-round control of the opponents' suit. For example:

♠ A 5
♡ A 10 3 2
◇ A K Q J 6
♣ 7 3

The bidding (your side vulnerable):

YOU	OPPONENT	PARTNER	OPPONENT
—	—	1 ♡	4 ♣
?			

You want to be in slam if partner can prevent the loss of the first two club tricks, and a jump to 5 ♡ will convey this message. And it hardly gives away any secrets, since your right-hand opponent is undoubtedly about to lead a club in any event.

Review Quiz

In each of the following problems, the vulnerability and bidding are shown. What call do you make?

(1) You are vulnerable

YOU	LHO	PARTNER	RHO
—	—	—	3 ◇
?			

You hold:
♠ K Q 10 5
♡ A K 7 6
◇ 8 4
♣ A J 9

(2) You are vulnerable

YOU	LHO	PARTNER	RHO	You hold:
—	—	—	4 ♣	♠ 6 4 3
?				♡ A 5
				◇ K 7 4 2
				♣ A Q 10 7

(3) Neither side vulnerable

YOU	LHO	PARTNER	RHO	You hold:
—	—	—	2 ♡*	♠ K 10 9 4
?				♡ 7 3
		*Weak Two-Bid		◇ A Q 10 6
				♣ K Q 3

(4) Neither side vulnerable

YOU	LHO	PARTNER	RHO	You hold:
—	—	—	2 ♠*	♠ K Q 10 8
?				♡ 5 2
		*Weak Two-Bid		◇ A 9 3
				♣ J 10 7 6

(5) You are vulnerable

YOU	LHO	PARTNER	RHO	You hold:
—	—	—	2 ♡*	♠ K 3
?				♡ K Q 5
		*Weak Two-Bid		◇ K 10 3 2
				♣ A Q 8 7

(6) Both sides vulnerable

YOU	LHO	PARTNER	RHO	You hold:
—	—	—	3 ♡	♠ A Q 9 8 6 3
?				♡ 5
				◇ A 9 6
				♣ K 10 3

(7) Both sides vulnerable

YOU	LHO	PARTNER	RHO	You hold:
—	—	Pass	3 ◇	♠ 6 2
?				♡ K Q 8 7 5
				◇ 7 4
				♣ A Q 6 3

(8) You are vulnerable

YOU	LHO	PARTNER	RHO	You hold:
—	—	—	4 ♡	♠ —
?				♡ 6 4
				◇ K Q 9 8 3 2
				♣ A K 9 7 6

(9) You are vulnerable

YOU	LHO	PARTNER	RHO	You hold:
—	Pass	Pass	4 ♠	♠ —
?				♡ Q J 10 6
				◇ K Q J 9 5
				♣ A Q J 3

(10) Both sides vulnerable

YOU	LHO	PARTNER	RHO	You hold:
—	—	—	4 ♠	♠ A Q 9 6
?				♡ A 6
				◇ 7 4 3 2
				♣ A 10 8

(11) You are vulnerable

YOU	LHO	PARTNER	RHO	You hold:
—	—	—	3 ◇	♠ A K 8
?				♡ A 3
				◇ 7 6 4 2
				♣ A Q 8 5

(12) Neither side vulnerable

YOU	LHO	PARTNER	RHO	You hold:
—	3 ◇	Pass	Pass	♠ A 9 7 3
?				♡ K Q 6
				◇ 4
				♣ K 10 8 6 4

(13) You are vulnerable

YOU	LHO	PARTNER	RHO	You hold:
—	—	—	3 ◇	♠ A 4
?				♡ A K J 9 6 3
				◇ 3 2
				♣ A Q J

(14) You are vulnerable

YOU	LHO	PARTNER	RHO	You hold:
—	3 ◇	3 ♠	Pass	♠ 6 4 2
?				♡ A 8 6
				◇ 9 6 4
				♣ Q 8 3 2

(15) You are vulnerable

YOU	LHO	PARTNER	RHO	You hold:
—	4 ♡	Double	Pass	♠ 7 3 2
?				♡ 8 6 4
				◇ A 8 4 2
				♣ K 7 5

(16) Both sides vulnerable

YOU	LHO	PARTNER	RHO	You hold:
—	3 ♣	3 ♡	Pass	♠ A 9 8 4
?				♡ K 8 6
				◇ Q 6 5 3 2
				♣ 7

(17) You are vulnerable

YOU	LHO	PARTNER	RHO	You hold:
Pass	3 ◇	Double	Pass	♠ Q 10 9 7 5
?				♡ 8 6
				◇ 7 4
				♣ K 9 8 6

(18) You are vulnerable

YOU	LHO	PARTNER	RHO	You hold:
Pass	3 ♣	Double	Pass	♠ 9 7 6
?				♡ 4 3 2
				◇ K 9 7 6 3
				♣ A Q

(19) You are vulnerable

YOU	LHO	PARTNER	RHO	You hold:
—	3 ◇	Double	Pass	♠ K 8 6 3
?				♡ A 7 4 2
				◇ 4
				♣ Q J 5 3

(20) Both sides vulnerable

YOU	LHO	PARTNER	RHO	You hold:
Pass	3 ♡	Double	Pass	♠ 7 6 4 3
?				♡ Q J 10 9
				◇ 6 4
				♣ A 6 3

Solutions

1. *Double.* You have more than the 16 points needed to bid at the three-level, good support for the unbid suits, and enough defensive strength to survive a pass by your part-

ner. Therefore the double is correct no matter whether you are using it as informatory, optional or for takeout.

2. *Pass.* You'll probably defeat 4 ♣, but you need a stronger hand to double a four-level preempt in case partner decides to bid something. Although penalty doubles work well in situations like this, they are losing strategy in the long run because you're more likely to need the double with hands that require cooperation from your partner. Besides, there is always the chance that he will balance with a double, enabling you to pass for penalties.

3. *Double.* Doubles of Weak Two-Bids are for takeout, and this hand meets all the requirements.

4. *Pass.* There is no good bid available, so wait and see if partner can take action.

5. *Two notrump.* This shows the equivalent of a strong no-trump opening bid (a balanced hand worth about 16-18 points) with stoppers in the enemy suit. With about 19-24 points you would jump to 3 NT. And if your right-hand opponent had opened with 3 ♡, you would overcall 3 NT, since a double could easily elicit an unwelcome spade response. Any of these bids could conceivably get you in trouble, but you must take some chances to overcome an enemy preempt when you have this much strength.

6. *Three spades.* Your hand is worth about 16 points, so show your fine spade suit; don't get finicky about a point or two when you have such clear-cut action at your disposal. A double is unlikely to succeed, as partner probably won't be able to bid spades even when you belong there.

7. *Pass.* You're too weak to bid at the three-level. To add to the general gloom, partner's original pass makes game for your side very unlikely and gives you even less reason to bid. But you should pass even if your right-hand opponent had been the dealer. Let your opponents take the huge sets by overbidding over *your* preempts, gracefully concede an occasional loss in situations like this, and you'll wind up well ahead in the long run.

8. *Four notrump.* You're more likely to have trouble finding the right trump suit after an enemy preempt than to care about the number of aces in partner's hand, so use the

4 NT overcall of a 4 ♡ preempt to ask partner to select his better minor suit.

9. *Four notrump.* Over a 4 ♠ preempt, the 4 NT overcall asks partner to choose among all three unbid suits.

10. *Double.* This is an exception to the general rule. Since the 4 NT overcall is available as a three-suited takeout over a 4 ♠ preempt, this particular double is for penalties regardless of what methods you are using. Thus you don't have to worry about an unwelcome bid by your partner.

11. *Double.* This is the best call *if* you are using informatory doubles, since you can show your considerable strength without risking a disastrous major-suit response on a mangy four-card suit. Using optional or takeout doubles, there is simply no good solution.

12. *Double.* Game is by no means out of reach, since partner may have had to pass with a fairly strong hand. You have good support for all unbid suits, and may act with about a trick less than usual when you are in balance position.

13. *Four hearts.* Don't risk partner passing a 3 ♡ overcall with a couple of high cards, as he will in accordance with the "Two Trick Rule," since you'll miss an excellent game.

14. *Pass.* After you discount your first two tricks or 6-8 points, as you should whenever partner enters the auction after an enemy preempt, you don't have anything left to justify a raise to game. If partner can make game opposite this mess, he should have bid more strongly.

15. *Pass.* "Stay fixed." There's no guarantee that you can find the right game contract at this level even if one exists, so take the sure profit. Perfectionists may occasionally reach a miracle contract after an enemy preempt, but they lose heavily in the long run.

16. *Four hearts.* You have more than the 6-8 points that partner is gambling on, so there is no reason to hang a trick short of game.

17. *Three spades.* Regardless of whether the double is informatory, optional, or for takeout, it's right to show your good major suit. Change the five of spades to the ace, however, and you should jump to 4 ♠.

18. *Three notrump.* At this vulnerability, declaring should be much more profitable than defending. Your club stoppers are more important than your long diamonds, since game in notrump requires two tricks less than game in a minor.
19. *Four diamonds.* You are strong enough to insist upon game, but selecting the wrong suit could cause a horrible disaster. You want partner to choose the contract, and this information can readily be conveyed by cue-bidding the opponents' suit.
20. *Pass.* Take the sure profit. You should be able to wreck the enemy contract even if your spade length causes some of partner's high cards to be ruffed away, and there is no guarantee that your side can make game. If your left-hand opponent has made a sketchy vulnerable preempt, the resulting penalty may keep him intimidated for the next six months.

5

Tactics and Conventions

♠ ♡ ◇ ♣

In this chapter we will consider some tactical situations and specialized bidding conventions that are of particular importance.

Preemptive Tactics

DON'T SAVE TWICE . . .

Once you have pushed the opponents into an awkward contract, it will usually be a good idea to let them suffer there. For example:

YOU	OPPONENT	PARTNER	OPPONENT
—	1 ♡	3 ♠	4 ♡
4 ♠	5 ♡	Pass	Pass
?			

In most cases you should pass. Your side's preemption has forced the opponents to make some difficult guesses, so they may be about to go down one in their awkward five-level contract; and partner will be highly irritated if you turn a plus score into a minus by stubbornly bidding 5 ♠. At worst, the opponents will make the same game that they would have registered at the four-level. "Heads you win, tails you tie" represents fine odds, so don't blow a good situation by telling the same story twice.

. . . BUT DO TAKE THE SMALL LOSS

When slams are involved, however, it is often a good idea to invest a few hundred points rather than risk a major catastrophe. Here's an example from the 1962 World Championships:

♠ Q 9 8 7 2
♡ Q 7
◊ —
♣ J 10 9 8 7 5

Neither side is vulnerable, and the auction proceeds:

YOU	OPPONENT	PARTNER	OPPONENT
—	—	1 ♠	5 ♡
5 ♠	Double	Pass	6 ♡
?			

The expert opponent on your right must have quite a hand to preempt at the five-level and then pull his partner's penalty double. If he thinks 5 ♠ doubled would have been good for your side, it can hardly be a disaster to pay out an extra 200 points; and allowing the enemy to make 6 ♡ could cost you the whole match. Therefore you should bid 6 ♠. If your left-hand opponent doubles and your right-hand opponent makes the extraordinary bid of 7 ♡, you should again take the small loss by bidding 7 ♠!* The complete deal:

---

*Unless partner is an expert, in which case you can safely pass the final decision around to him. He'll take the save unless he has a sure trick against 7 ♡.

NORTH
♠ J 10 5
♡ —
◇ A Q J 10 6 4
♣ A 4 3 2

WEST (you)   EAST
♠ Q 9 8 7 2   ♠ A K 6 4 3
♡ Q 7   ♡ 9
◇ —   ◇ K 9 8 7 2
♣ J 10 9 8 7 5   ♣ Q 6

SOUTH
♠ —
♡ A K J 10 8 6 5 4 3 2
◇ 5 3
♣ K

Admittedly, this is an extreme example. But usually it will be an excellent idea to avoid trying to make pinpoint decisions at slam levels. If good opponents keep bidding, and especially if the vulnerability is favorable, make sure you buy the contract when freak hands abound. You may throw away several hundred points on any one deal, but you'll save thousands in the long run.

THE STRATEGIC UNDERBID

Although it is usually a good idea to make your maximum preempt at once, there are some occasions when strategy may dictate an alternative course of action. Suppose that partner opens with 3 ◇ and you hold:

♠ 3 2
♡ 5
◇ J 9 7 6 5
♣ J 10 9 8 7

It certainly looks as though the opponents can make a grand slam. So, depending on the vulnerability, a jump to 6 ◇ or even 7 ◇ is not unreasonable. However, bidding grand slams is not all that easy even when they turn out to be laydown, and a high-level preempt could push the opponents into the very contract that you fear. Therefore some experts would bid only 4 ◇ or 5 ◇, or perhaps even pass, hoping that the opponents will stop too low if left to their own devices. In truth, there is no "right answer" in this situation, and experience plus a sense of what is going on at the table must determine the final choice.

The strategic underbid also arises in unusual situations like this:

♠ 3
♡ K Q 10 8 6 4
◇ —
♣ A K 9 8 6 5

Your side is vulnerable, and partner deals and opens with 1 ♡. A direct jump to 6 ♡ could not be criticized, but it is likely to goad your opponents into taking the sacrifice that you know will be very cheap (probably less than even the value of your *game*). Therefore some theorists would start off with only 2 ♡ or 3 ♡ and keep bidding very slowly, figuring that they will be ahead if they buy the hand at *any* level—and that the wild distribution will keep the auction going for quite a while, making the strategic underbid a safe choice. The complete deal might well be:

NORTH (you)
♠ 3
♡ K Q 10 8 6 4
♢ —
♣ A K 9 8 6 5

WEST
♠ A 10 8 6 5
♡ —
♢ A J 10 9 8
♣ 10 4 3

EAST
♠ K J 9 7 2
♡ 3 2
♢ 7 5 3 2
♣ Q 7

SOUTH (partner)
♠ Q 4
♡ A J 9 7 5
♢ K Q 6 4
♣ J 2

Although you are cold for 6 ♡, you would rather play in 4 ♡ and make 680 than have the opponents sacrifice in 6 ♠ and pay you only 300. If you bid the hand slowly, giving the impression that you have been pushed into slam against your will, the opponents might elect to defend against 6 ♡:

SOUTH	WEST	NORTH	EAST
1 ♡	1 ♠	2 ♡ (!)	4 ♠
Pass	Pass	5 ♡	Pass
Pass	5 ♠	6 ♡	??
	??		

They *should* take the save, in accordance with the precept of buying a freak hand at any cost, but there is every chance that they will go wrong.

The strategic underbid is also used by some players when their opponents open the bidding and they have a solid nine-card or ten-card suit. Intead of preempting, they start with a simple overcall and continue to bid as slowly as possible in the hope of stealing the contract.

In the last two situations, the repeated bids of your suit may well give the show away to a knowledgeable opponent. A strategic underbid in response to partner's opening preempt is more likely to succeed, however, since you are behaving just as you would with some defensive values—raising a level or two at your first turn and passing thereafter.

THE COMPETITIVE DOUBLE

Suppose that both sides are vulnerable and you deal yourself:

♠ 2
♡ A K J 10 8 7 6 5
♢ A 4
♣ 7 6

You elect to open with 4 ♡, your left-hand opponent overcalls with 4 ♠, and the next two players pass. What now?

Ordinarily, it is wrong for a preempter to bid again, but this is an exceptional case. Your hand is worth a probable nine tricks, and hence a five-level contract is fully justified; all that stopped you from bidding more at your first turn was the fact that opening bids of five of a *major* are *not* used as preempts. But why put all your eggs in one basket by bidding 5 ♡? Partner may well have a couple of spade tricks and a card or two on the side, yet have been unable to double 4 ♠ because he didn't expect you to have any defensive values.

A better plan is to double. This shows that you would like to go on to 5 ♡, but that you have as much defensive strength *as can reasonably be expected in view of your opening preempt* and won't mind if partner passes for penalties with a spade stack. If partner's defensive strength is at best dubious, he is expected to remove your double to 5 ♡ rather than risk disaster.

THE PSYCHIC 3 NT RESPONSE

If the vulnerability is favorable, partner opens with 3 ♣ or 3 ◇ and the next player passes, and you have some support for his suit but are fairly broke otherwise, one good procedure is to raise his suit to a very high level. An alternative old trick, still effective in some quarters, is to respond 3 NT. If the opponents believe that you have a strong hand and let you play there, you'll come out well ahead, for even going down six or seven will be better than letting them make their cold game (or slam). And if they double, you can speedily return to partner's suit.

Here's an example, based on a hand from an expert team match played in 1965:

North dealer
East-West vulnerable

```
                    NORTH
                    ♠  5 4
                    ♡  9 7
                    ◇  Q J 4
                    ♣  K Q J 10 9 6
WEST                                      EAST
♠  Q 10 7 3                               ♠  A K J 9 8
♡  K 8 6 5 2                               ♡  J 3
◇  K 7                                     ◇  A 10 8 6
♣  4 2                                     ♣  5 3
                    SOUTH
                    ♠  6 2
                    ♡  A Q 10 4
                    ◇  9 5 3 2
                    ♣  A 8 7
```

The bidding:

SOUTH	WEST	NORTH	EAST
—	—	3 ♣	Pass
3 NT	Pass	Pass	Pass

The opponents took the first seven tricks, so South went down three. But he was perfectly satisfied to pay out 150 points, for the opponents could have chalked up 620 by bidding and making 4 ♠.

THE PSYCHIC 4 NT RESPONSE

Another well-known subterfuge is to camouflage an advance sacrifice as a Blackwood slam try. For example, suppose that partner opens with 3 ♡ at favorable vulnerability, the next player passes, and you hold:

♠ 3
♡ 9 8 7 6
♢ A 6 4 2
♣ A 7 4 3

The opponents can undoubtedly make a lot of spades, so emergency action is called for. One good solution is to jump directly to 6 ♡, taking what should be a profitable advance sacrifice and giving the opponents a chance to go wrong at a high level of bidding. A possible alternative is to respond 4 NT, planning to stop in 5 ♡ regardless of the number of aces partner turns up with. If the opponents are conned into thinking that you have a strong hand, they may double you a level too low—or perhaps even neglect to double at all. The potential cost is that if they are able to get to 5 ♠ anyway, your subsequent 6 ♡ sacrifice will be somewhat easier for them to cope with because they have already had an opportunity to exchange some information.

THE PSYCHIC RESPONSE IN A NEW SUIT

When holding a weak hand opposite partner's opening preempt, some experts try to bluff their opponents by bidding a weak suit. If they are doubled, they simply return to opener's suit. This psychic response can be effective, but should be tried only by very experienced players.

Preemptive Conventions

Because high-level bids can be so effective, many players use special bidding methods that enable them to preempt more often. Some of these conventions have considerable merit, while others are of a more debatable nature.

TRANSFER PREEMPTS

Although preempting with an absolutely solid major suit is quite safe, it could lead to a missed slam because partner does not expect you to have so many top tricks. To avoid preempting themselves into a state of confusion, some experts use the following convention:

Opening Bid	*Meaning*
4 ♠	Ordinary preempt with broken suit.
4 ♡	Ordinary preempt with broken suit.
4 ◇	Strong 4 ♠ preempt with solid spades, and perhaps even some outside high cards. Shows interest in slam.
4 ♣	Strong 4 ♡ preempt.
3 NT	Ordinary 4 ♣ or 4 ◇ preempt.

After a 3 NT opening bid, responder must not pass unless he has a powerful hand and expects to make game in notrump opposite an ordinary four-level preempt. He bids 4 ♣ with no interest in game and 5 ♣ if he does wish to play in game, and opener corrects to diamonds if that is his suit. Over a 4 ♣ opening bid, responder bids 4 ◇ if he has no interest in slam and passes partner's return to 4 ♡. (It is usually best to make the preempter the declarer, so that the defenders cannot see which side suit to attack.) With slam expectations, responder can cue-bid an ace, jump directly to slam if he has side-suit holdings that should be led up to, or bid 4 ◇ and then raise to 6 ♡ if he wants opener to declare the contract. Responses to a 4 ◇ opening bid follow a similar strategy.

Transfer preempts have several advantages. They may enable you to reach an excellent 3 NT contract that would have been missed had a normal 4 ♣ or 4 ◇ opening bid been made. Or they may pick up a swing by allowing you to start and stop at the four-level instead of exploring for a hopeless slam and letting the opponents get into the act, as in this deal from the 1969 U.S. Spring National Team of Four Championships:

North dealer
Neither side vulnerable

```
                        NORTH
                        ♠  8
                        ♡  9 4 2
                        ◇  Q 10 3
                        ♣  J 10 7 6 3 2
WEST                                        EAST
♠  J 10 9 4                                 ♠  A K 7 5 3
♡  3                                        ♡  10 5
◇  A K J 4 2                                ◇  9 7 6 5
♣  K 8 4                                    ♣  9 5
                        SOUTH
                        ♠  Q 6 2
                        ♡  A K Q J 8 7 6
                        ◇  8
                        ♣  A Q
```

The bidding, Room 1:

SOUTH	WEST	NORTH	EAST
		Pass	Pass
4 ♣	Pass	4 ◊	Pass
4 ♡	Pass	Pass	Pass

The bidding, Room 2:

SOUTH	WEST	NORTH	EAST
		Pass	Pass
1 ♡	Double	2 ♡	3 ♠
4 ♡	4 ♠	Pass	Pass
5 ♡	Pass	Pass	Pass

In Room 1, South used a transfer preempt of 4 ♣ to shut out the opponents and express a strong interest in slam, and was able to stop just in time when his partner used the signoff sequence. In Room 2, however, the 1 ♡ opening bid was mandatory because transfer preempts were not being used and the hand was far too strong for a regular preempt. That low bid enabled the opponents to contest the auction and make thorough nuisances of themselves. North and South quite reasonably chose to push on to 5 ♡, and wound up with a minus score when the defenders cashed their aces and the club finesse failed.

Transfer preempts also have some important disadvantages. They are very easy to forget; and if partner thinks you have long clubs when you actually have a vast number of hearts (or vice versa), the ensuing catastrophe may ruin your whole evening (or match). In addition, transfer preempts provide the opponents with extra methods for entering the auction, and are therefore somewhat easier to compete against than are standard four-level preempts. Here's one good defensive method.

Double of 4 ♣ or 4 ◊ = about 14-17 points, guarantees support
    for the other major. Takeout oriented, but partner may double

the opponents' real suit for penalties with a couple of defensive tricks and no good bid to make.

Overcall in opener's real (major) suit = About 18 points or more, guarantees support for the other major and at least one other suit.

Pass, then double opener's real (major) suit = Good hand, relatively balanced, inferior support for the other major. Penalty oriented, but partner should bid with a good suit of his own, control of opener's real suit, and slam aspirations.

4 NT = Minor-suit takeout.

Suit overcalls (including opener's minor) = Natural bids.

Using this approach, the West player in the preceding deal could have doubled 4 ♣ and enabled East to bid 4 ♠. For many players, therefore, the defects of transfer preempts outweigh the advantages.

PREEMPTIVE JUMP RAISES OF OVERCALLS

If partner overcalls an enemy opening bid of one of a suit, you can show a strong hand by cue-bidding. Therefore it's a good idea to use jump raises of overcalls as preemptive bids. For example, suppose that the player on your left opens with 1 ♣, partner overcalls with 1 ♡, the next player passes, and you hold (neither side vulnerable):

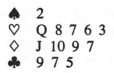

♠   2
♡   Q 8 7 6 3
♢   J 10 9 7
♣   9 7 5

Using preemptive raises of overcalls, you should bid 3 ♡. This will make it hard for the opponents to locate their probable spade fit, and a serious penalty is unlikely in view of your fine heart support.

With good support for partner's suit and a strong hand, act as follows:

6- 9 points: Make a single raise of partner's suit.

10-12 points: Cue-bid the enemy suit, then support partner's suit at the *two*-level (or pass if he rebids two of his suit).

13-15 points: Cue-bid the enemy suit, then support partner's suit at the *three*-level or higher. (*Don't* pass!)

Be sure to note that after a cue-bid, the overcaller must *not* rebid just two of his suit if he sees a chance for game opposite a 10-12 point hand, as the cue-bidder will pass with that holding.

To illustrate, suppose the partner's 1 ♡ overcall of the enemy 1 ♣ opening bid finds you with either of these hands:

(a)	♠	A 10 6 2	(b)	♠	A 10 6 2
	♡	J 9 8 7		♡	Q 9 8 7
	◇	K Q 3		◇	A Q 9
	♣	9 7		♣	9 7

Since a jump raise would show a weak hand, you must first cue-bid 2 ♣. With hand (a), correct a 2 ◇ rebid to 2 ♡, or pass if partner rebids 2 ♡. With hand (b), however, bid at least 3 ♡ at your next turn to show 13-15 points.

At times, desperate measures (in the form of an advance sacrifice) may be necessary when your hand is weak. Examine this deal (opponents vulnerable):

YOU	OPPONENT	PARTNER	OPPONENT
—	1 ♠	2 ♡	2 ♠
?			

Suppose you hold:

♠ 7 5 4 2
♡ K 8 6 5 2
♢ 10 5 3
♣ 6

You should jump to 5 ♡, taking what is likely to be a good sacrifice against the opponents' vulnerable spade game and making them guess what to do at the five-level. Partner must be very short in spades, since the suit has been bid and raised and you have four of them, so your hands will fit extremely well. For example, you'll get out for down two even if he has as little as:

♠ 3
♡ A Q J 9 7
♢ 7 6 4
♣ A 9 8 3

It is interesting to note, however, that the following hand is worth only a preemptive jump raise to 4 ♡:

♠ 6
♡ K 8 6 5 2
♢ 10 5 3
♣ 7 5 4 2

Although similar to the first example, this hand will produce several fewer tricks if partner is also short in spades. And your spade shortness suggests that he just might have a trump stack and be thirsting to double the opponents. Thus there is every reason to content yourself with suggesting a sacrifice and leave the final decision to your partner.

PREEMPTIVE JUMP SHIFTS IN COMPETITION

In standard bidding, a jump shift response to partner's opening bid of one of a suit (such as a 2 ♡ response to a 1 ♣ opening bid) is forcing to game and shows a very powerful hand. Some experts have suggested that this bid be used instead as a weak preempt, but this approach makes it rather difficult to bid slams with any accuracy when you have a strong hand.

If partner's opening bid has been overcalled by your right-hand opponent, however, it is reasonable to use a jump shift response as preemptive. To illustrate, suppose that your partner opens with 1 ♣, the next player overcalls with 1 ♢, and you hold (neither side vulnerable):

```
♠   7
♡   Q 9 7 6 4 3 2
♢   8 6 3
♣   5 4
```

If you are using preemptive jump shifts in competition, you can show your long suit and warn partner that you are virtually broke by jumping to 2 ♡. Using standard methods, you would either have to pass (since you lack the high-card strength for a 1 ♡ response) or risk preempting at a high level with a weak suit.

PREEMPTIVE JUMPS OVER A TAKEOUT DOUBLE

If partner opens with one of a suit and the next player doubles, you can show a strong hand by redoubling. Therefore it's desirable to use jumps in a new suit, or jump raises of partner's suit, as

preemptive bids. For example, suppose that partner opens with
1 ♣, the next player doubles, and you hold any of these hands
(neither side vulnerable):

(a)	(b)	(c)
♠ Q J 10 8 7 6	♠ 7 6 3	♠ J 7 6 4 3 2
♡ 3	♡ 4	♡ 8 2
◇ 6 4 2	◇ Q 8 3 2	◇ 7 6 3
♣ J 9 8	♣ J 10 9 8 6	♣ K 8

Bid 2 ♠ with hand (a). This shows a strong suit and very little
outside strength, and advises partner to pass unless he has a powerhouse with support for your suit. Change a small diamond to a
small spade, giving you a seven-card suit, and you should respond
3 ♠.

With hand (b) respond 3 ♣. This should be safe even if partner
has a three-card club suit, and will make your opponents' task
considerably more difficult.

If you have hand (c), however, you should pass. It is dangerous
to preempt with a weak suit, for your right-hand opponent's an-
nouncement that he has support for all unbid suits will make it easy
for his partner to double for penalties. Since the doubler is likely to
have four spades, you're probably best off out of the auction.

Pseudo-Preempts

In standard bidding, *double* jump shift responses to partner's
opening bid of one of a suit are used as preemptive bids. For example, a 4 ◇ response to partner's 1 ♡ opening bid shows something
like eight diamonds to the queen and very little outside strength.
Similar meanings apply to auctions like 1 ♣—3 ♠, 1 ♠—4 ♣,
1 ♡—3 ♠, 1 ◇—4 ♣, and so on.

Since the opportunity to use these responses as preempts arises
very rarely, modern experts prefer to use them as conventional bids.
One current approach, called Splinter Bids, has considerable merit
and enjoys widespread popularity among experts.

SPLINTER BIDS

. When your side is in the slam range, it can be extremely important to know whether or not partner has a singleton—and *where* his singleton happens to be. To illustrate, 6 ♠ will be laydown if your combined holding is:

(a)

YOU	PARTNER
♠ A Q J 6 5	♠ K 10 7 4 3
♡ K 3	♡ A 7 5 2
◇ 9 6 3	◇ 8
♣ K Q 4	♣ A 7 2

However, you could easily be held to just 4 ♠ if your side has:

(b)

YOU	PARTNER
♠ A Q J 6 5	♠ K 10 7 4 3
♡ K 3	♡ A 7 5 2
◇ 9 6 3	◇ A 7 2
♣ K Q 4	♣ 8

The total point count is the same in both cases; the only difference is the location of partner's singleton. In example (b), your side suffers from *duplication of values*. Partner's singleton clashes with your king and queen of clubs, so neither holding turns out to be worth its full value. In example (a), however, all of your high cards are "working" because you have only small cards opposite partner's singleton. As a result, you can make *two* tricks more—and a slam.

There is more to bidding than simply counting points, and it is often essential to determine whether or not your values are actually pulling their full weight. Therefore many experts use Splinter Bids to resolve such vexing problems. Here's how they work: After partner opens with one of a *major* suit, a double jump shift shows a *singleton* in the bid suit, four-card or longer support for opener's suit, and 13-15 points (the equivalent of a strong double raise). In example (a) the auction would proceed:

YOU	PARTNER
1 ♠	4 ◇ (a)
4 NT (b)	5 ♡
6 ♠	Pass

(a)   Splinter Bid showing a singleton diamond, four-card or longer spade support, and 13-15 points.
(b)   Ordinarily it is incorrect to use Blackwood with two or three quick losers in a side suit, as the opponents might be able to take the first two tricks in that suit if partner turns up with the "wrong" aces. Here, however, you can bid as though you had a singleton diamond.

Case (b) would be handled as follows:

YOU	PARTNER
1 ♠	4 ♣ (a)
4 ♠ (b)	Pass

(a)   Splinter Bid.
(b)   Your king and queen of clubs are worth less than usual now that partner has turned up with a singleton, so you have a minimum opening bid—and no reason to try for slam.

To show a void, responder starts off with a Splinter Bid. Then he bids his short suit again at his next turn if he can do so at a safe level.

Splinter Bids are extremely valuable, and are strongly recommended for your use. In fact, they are so helpful that some experts use *any unusual* jump shift as a Splinter Bid, no matter when it may occur during the auction.

VOID-SHOWING RESPONSES

Since showing void suits can be awkward when using Splinter Bids, a few theorists prefer to play that the double jump shift response guarantees a void in the bid suit. For example:

(a) **Opener**

♠ A K Q 8 6
♡ K Q 3
◇ 7 6 3
♣ K 7

Responder

♠ J 9 7 3 2
♡ A 8 5 2
◇ —
♣ A 9 8 4

Opener starts off with 1 ♠, and responder bids 4 ◇ to show a void in diamonds, 13-15 points,* and four-card or longer spade support. It is now a simple matter for opener to use Blackwood and promptly bid 7 ♠ when responder turns up with two aces in addition to his diamond void.

(b) **Opener**

♠ A K Q 8 6
♡ K Q 3
◇ 7 6 3
♣ K 7

Responder

♠ J 9 7 3 2
♡ A 8 5 2
◇ A 9 8 4
♣ —

In this case, the auction would proceed:

Opener	Responder
1 ♠	4 ♣
4 ♠	Pass

*Remember that a void together with excellent support for partner's suit is worth 5 points, and a singleton is worth 3 points.

After the void-showing response, opener knows that his king of clubs is useless. If responder has enough red-suit strength for slam, he will surely act again over the 4 ♠ rebid.

While void-showing responses may prove superior in some situations, Splinter Bids figure to be more effective in the long run because crucial singletons are more frequent occurrences than crucial voids. And Splinter Bids could well reach the right spot even in the above examples:

(a)	*Opener*	*Responder*	(b)	*Opener*	*Responder*
	1 ♠	4 ◇		1 ♠	4 ♣
	4 NT	5 ♡		4 ♠	5 ♣
	6 ◇!	7 ♠		5 ♠	Pass
	Pass				

Responder does not get a chance to rebid 5 ◇ to show his void in example (a), but opener's ingenuity comes to the rescue. He can hardly want to play opposite responder's short suit when an excellent spade fit is known to exist, so he must be asking responder to stop in 6 ♠ with a singleton diamond and go on to 7 ♠ with a void in diamonds. Admittedly this is a rather difficult auction, and it would not even be possible if the clubs and diamonds were switched because a 6 ♣ rebid would be the Delayed Grand Slam Force.

In example (b), responder shows his void in clubs by rebidding 5 ♣ after his initial Splinter Bid. Opener is still not interested in slam because three of his high-card points are wasted, and the partnership stops just in time.

SWISS

Some players use the jump response of four of a minor to an opening bid of 1 ♡ or 1 ♠ to show a strong double raise with an important additional feature. For example, the 4 ◇ response may guarantee either three aces or two aces and the king of trumps, while 4 ♣ shows poorer controls. Or 4 ◇ may promise unusually powerful trump support and 4 ♣ may show excellent controls (or vice versa). Although formerly popular, Swiss has largely been superseded by Splinter Bids among today's top players.

ASKING BIDS

A few theorists use double jump responses as asking bids, inquiring about partner's holding in the bid suit (and perhaps his other values as well). For example, these responses could be used as Control Asking Bids (see Chapter 3), or as highly complex requests for detailed information about opener's hand. However, Splinter Bids are likely to be more useful as well as easier on your memory.

Play after a Preempt

Although this is a book about bidding, it is worth noting that the impact of a preemptive bid does not end when the auction is over. If the opponents preempt and buy the contract and you are on opening lead, special tactics are likely to be necessary. On the other hand, if you manage to overcome an enemy preempt and become the declarer, you had best keep the preempt firmly in mind while you are planning your line of play.

OPENING LEADS

It is frequently desirable to try to cash tricks quickly after an enemy preempt has bought the contract, especially if the partner of the preemptive bidder has raised to game. For example:

♠ A 10 3
♡ J 4 2
◇ K J
♣ 10 9 8 7 4

The bidding (opponents are vulnerable):

YOU	OPPONENT	PARTNER	OPPONENT
—	—	—	3 ♠
Pass	4 ♠	Pass	Pass
Pass			

Partner's silence, the vulnerability, and your meager assets suggest that your left-hand opponent is raising to game because he expects to make it. As we observed in Chapter 3, this implies that he has a hand rich in top tricks, so declarer is likely to be able to discard some losers on dummy's aces and kings unless you get there first by cashing your own winners. You can tell from your hand that your side's most likely source of tricks is in diamonds, so you should lead the king of diamonds. Here's the complete deal, which arose in a New York tournament:

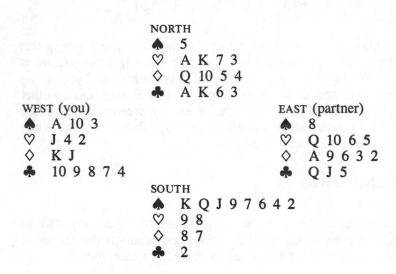

```
                    NORTH
                    ♠  5
                    ♡  A K 7 3
                    ◊  Q 10 5 4
                    ♣  A K 6 3
WEST (you)                              EAST (partner)
♠  A 10 3                               ♠  8
♡  J 4 2                                ♡  Q 10 6 5
◊  K J                                  ◊  A 9 6 3 2
♣  10 9 8 7 4                           ♣  Q J 5
                    SOUTH
                    ♠  K Q J 9 7 6 4 2
                    ♡  9 8
                    ◊  8 7
                    ♣  2
```

Your king of diamonds wins the first trick, and you continue with a diamond to partner's ace. He plays a third round of diamonds, and this defeats the contract. If declarer ruffs low, you will overruff; if South ruffs with an honor, you will discard and subsequently win two trump tricks. After a club or heart lead, however, declarer simply discards a losing diamond on one of dummy's high clubs before drawing trumps and proceeds to make his contract with an overtrick.

Be careful, however, not to carry this useful principle too far. Suppose you hold:

♠ 5 4 3
♡ A 7 3
◊ 8 6 4 2
♣ K Q J

If your right-hand opponent opens with 3 ♠ and his partner raises to 4 ♠, lead the king of clubs. Cashing the heart ace will enable declarer to get rid of some club losers in a hurry if dummy turns up with the king and queen of hearts.

DECLARER PLAY

If one of your opponents has made a preemptive bid, he must have a great many cards in his suit. Therefore he is likely to be short in the other suits, and you are likely to encounter bad splits when you attempt to bring home your contract. All too many players forget about a preempt after the auction is over and blithely play for 2-2, 3-2, or other "normal" divisions, in spite of the fact that the preemptive bid has virtually announced that abnormal things are going to happen. As a result, they go down in games or slams that could easily have been made. Here's a sad example:

NORTH
♠ K 10 9 8
♡ A 4
◊ 5 4 3 2
♣ A K Q

SOUTH
♠ A J 7 5 4
♡ 2
◊ A K Q 10
♣ 8 3 2

The bidding (both sides vulnerable):

SOUTH	WEST	NORTH	EAST
—	3 ♡	Double	4 ♡
6 ♠	Pass	Pass	Pass

West led the jack of clubs, and declarer, who "knew" that the percentages favored playing for the drop with nine trumps in the combined hands, quickly cashed the king and ace of spades. He blinked when the queen of spades failed to drop, turned green when West later turned up with four diamonds to the jack, and unhappily paid out 100 points.

South blew about 1500 points on this deal, for the small slam is virtually laydown. West is marked with at least a seven-card suit for his vulnerable preempt, and he must have at least one club in view of his opening lead (no doubt a singleton, desperately hoping that East has the ace and will give him a ruff). If he also has two or more spades, he can't possibly have enough diamonds to present any problems. Therefore the right play is to cash the king of spades and lead the ten, planning to finesse if East follows with a small spade. Here's the complete deal:

```
                    NORTH
                    ♠  K 10 9 8
                    ♡  A 4
                    ◇  5 4 3 2
                    ♣  A K Q
WEST                                      EAST
♠  2                                      ♠  Q 6 3
♡  K Q J 9 8 7 6                          ♡  10 5 3
◇  J 9 8 7                                ◇  6
♣  J                                      ♣  10 9 7 6 5 4
                    SOUTH
                    ♠  A J 7 5 4
                    ♡  2
                    ◇  A K Q 10
                    ♣  8 3 2
```

The moral: *Don't* expect ordinary suit splits after one of your opponents has made a preemptive bid!

Review Quiz

In each of the following problems, the vulnerability and bidding are shown. What call do you make?

(1) Opponents are vulnerable

YOU	LHO	PARTNER	RHO	You hold:
—	1 ♠	4 ♣	4 ♠	♠ 3
5 ♣	5 ♠	Pass	Pass	♡ Q J 4 3
?				◇ A 9 6 5 2
				♣ K 8 7

(2) Opponents are vulnerable

YOU	LHO	PARTNER	RHO	You hold:
—	—	1 ♠	4 ♡	♠ K 9 8 7 3
4 ♠	Pass	Pass	5 ♡	♡ 10
5 ♠	Double	Pass	6 ♡	◇ J 10 9 7 6 4 3
?				♣ —

(3) Opponents are vulnerable

YOU	LHO	PARTNER	RHO	You hold:
—	—	Pass	Pass	♠ A K J 9 7 6 4 3
4 ♠	5 ♣	Pass	Pass	♡ A 5
?				◇ 6 4
				♣ 2

(4) Opponents are vulnerable

YOU	LHO	PARTNER	RHO	You hold:
—	—	3 ♣	Double	♠ 4 3
?				♡ 8 5 3
				♢ 4 2
				♣ J 9 7 6 3 2

(5) Neither side vulnerable

YOU	LHO	PARTNER	RHO	You hold:
—	1 ♢	2 ♣	Pass	♠ 2
?				♡ 4 2
				♢ 10 9 8 6 3
				♣ Q J 7 6 5

(6) Neither side vulnerable

YOU	LHO	PARTNER	RHO	You hold:
—	—	1 ♡	Double	♠ 3
?				♡ 4 2
				♢ Q J 9 8 7 5 4
				♣ 10 7 6

(7) Opponents are vulnerable

YOU	LHO	PARTNER	RHO	You hold:
—	—	—	4 ♣*	♠ A 8 6 5
?				♡ 3
		*Transfer preempt showing		♢ A 5 4 2
		strong hearts and slam		♣ K Q 10 6
		interest		

(8) Both sides vulnerable

YOU	LHO	PARTNER	RHO	You hold:
—	—	1 ♠	Pass	♠ Q 9 8 6
?				♡ A 10 3 2
				◇ 2
				♣ A 10 8 5

(9) Both sides vulnerable

YOU	LHO	PARTNER	RHO	You hold:
1 ♠	Pass	4 ♣*	Pass	♠ A J 8 6 3
?				♡ A 8 5
		*Splinter Bid		◇ K 2
				♣ K J 4

(10) Both sides vulnerable

YOU	LHO	PARTNER	RHO	You hold:
1 ♠	Pass	4 ♣*	Pass	♠ A J 8 6 3
?				♡ A K J
		*Splinter Bid		◇ K 4
				♣ 8 6 3

Solutions

1. *Pass*. Let the opponents suffer in their awkward five-level contract. If they go down one, your preemptive tactics will have scored a handsome gain; if they do manage to struggle home with their contract, they'll make only the same

game that they would have registered at the four-level. "Heads you win, tails you tie" offers unusually good odds, so don't pass it up.

2. *Six spades*. Something very unusual is going on, and it's good strategy to insist upon buying the contract when freak hands are likely to be on the loose. If your vulnerable opponent doesn't want you to play in 5 ♠ doubled, investing a potential 200 points extra by bidding 6 ♠ can hardly turn out to be a disaster. Here's the complete deal:

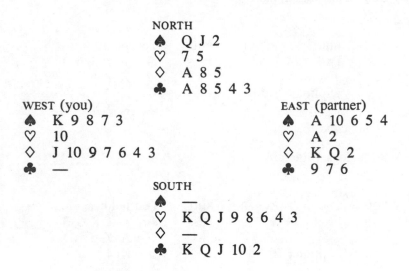

NORTH
♠ Q J 2
♡ 7 5
◇ A 8 5
♣ A 8 5 4 3

WEST (you)
♠ K 9 8 7 3
♡ 10
◇ J 10 9 7 6 4 3
♣ —

EAST (partner)
♠ A 10 6 5 4
♡ A 2
◇ K Q 2
♣ 9 7 6

SOUTH
♠ —
♡ K Q J 9 8 6 4 3
◇ —
♣ K Q J 10 2

You may not agree with South's strategic underbids, but you'll still have to pay him about 1400 points if you allow him to play in 6 ♡. But 6 ♠ doubled goes for a mere 100 despite the bad (although predictable) trump break.

3. *Double*. Actually, a 1 ♠ opening bid is likely to be superior when you have this much defensive strength (and the highest-ranking suit), but you can recoup by making the right bid now. The double shows as much defensive strength as partner could possibly expect in view of your preempt, and indicates that you are not yet ready to give up

the fight. Partner is asked to pass with good defensive values, but to bid 5 ♠ if a trick or two from your hand does not figure to be enough to defeat the enemy contract.

4. *Four clubs, five clubs, six clubs, seven clubs, pass, three notrump or four notrump.* And if you don't care for any of these choices, a side-suit psychic bid is also acceptable. The problem with a jump to 7 ♣ is that it may well push the opponents into a grand slam that you very much fear will be laydown. Therefore a strategic underbid of 4 ♣ or 5 ♣ might work well—but there is really no right answer in a situation like this. Experience, a knowledge of your opponents, and luck must decide the issue.

5. *Four clubs,* assuming you are using preemptive raises of overcalls. This useful convention enables you to make life difficult for the opponents while warning partner to proceed with caution. Using standard methods, you must choose between a pass (which gives the opponents a free run) and a raise to 3 ♣ (which may get partner overly excited and your side too high.)

6. *Three diamonds.* You would redouble with a strong hand, so the jump response is preemptive in nature.

7. *Double.* After an ordinary four-level preempt, you would reluctantly have to pass. Here, however, the opponents do not intend to play in clubs, so you can let partner know that you have a light takeout double of the real enemy suit —hearts.

8. *Four diamonds using Splinter Bids, three spades using standard methods.* Counting three points for the singleton in support of partner's suit, your hand is worth a forcing raise to game. In standard methods, the 4 ◇ response is used as a very weak preeempt; but hands requiring this bid arise so rarely that most experts have switched to conventional approaches. And the most popular (and best) approach is the Splinter Bid, showing a strong major raise with a singleton or void in the bid suit.

9. *Four spades.* Your club honors will be virtually worthless opposite partner's small singleton, so you have no reason to try for slam.

10. *Four notrump.* This time all of your high cards are "working"; none are wasted opposite partner's short suit. There-

fore it's time to check for aces and head for slam. Partner's hand:

♠ K Q 10 4
♥ Q 6 4 2
♦ A 8 7 6
♣ 5

Note that slam is icy, while you could easily be held to just 4 ♠ in the preceding problem—and your side's point count is the same in both cases.